PR5631.E46 1971

1245031

T.C.J.C.-S.C.

SOUTH CAMPUS LIBRARY

TARRANT COUNTY JUNIOR COLLEGE

FT. WORTH, TEXAS 76119

THACKERAY

THACKERAY
by G. U. ELLIS

Great Lives

HASKELL HOUSE PUBLISHERS Ltd.
Publishers of Scarce Scholarly Books
NEW YORK, N. Y. 10012
1971

First Published 1933

HASKELL HOUSE PUBLISHERS LTD.
Publishers of Scarce Scholarly Books
280 LAFAYETTE STREET
NEW YORK. N. Y. 10012

Library of Congress Catalog Card Number: 79-160465

Standard Book Number 8383-1300-0

Printed in the United States of America

CONTENTS

Chapter I . . . . . *page* 9
Ancestry – parentage – birth – school – university – Dr. Maginn and Bohemia – inheritance.

Chapter II 23
" Wild oats " – newspaper ventures – the last of the patrimony – *Fraser's Magazine* – Bulwer-baiting – marriage – hack-journalism – Yellowplush and Michael Angelo Titmarsh – wife's insanity.

Chapter III 45
Bachelor life in London – *Paris Sketch Book* – Charles Lever and *Irish Sketch Book* – *Punch* – *From Cornhill to Cairo* – literary quarrels – *The Luck of Barry Lyndon*.

Chapter IV 62
The Brookfields and their circle – Thackeray and Mrs. Brookfield – *Jeames's Diary* – *The Book of Snobs* – Carlyle's opinion of Thackeray – the first number of *Vanity Fair*.

Chapter V 74
Accusations of snobbery – his children join him in London – the slow progress of *Vanity Fair* – Charlotte Brontë's dedication of *Jane Eyre* to Thackeray – scandal and success.

Chapter VI 87
Relations between Thackeray and Dickens – the effect of Dickens' work on Thackeray's – increasing popularity – quarrel with Charles Lever – *Pendennis* – illness – accusations of lampooning old *Fraserian* colleagues.

CONTENTS

Chapter VII . . . . . *page* 100

The English Humourists – quarrel with the Brookfields – *Esmond* commissioned – differences with and resignation from *Punch* – sails for America.

Chapter VIII 111

The first American tour – ill health – *The Newcomes* – *The Four Georges* and the second American tour – stands for Parliament at Oxford and is defeated – *The Virginians*.

Chapter IX 125

The Yates affair – quarrel with Dickens – opinions on *The Virginians* – the editorship of the *Cornhill* – relations with Trollope – increasing illness – *Lovel the Widower* and *Philip* – back to the eighteenth century with *Denis Duval* – the last quarrel – death.

CHRONOLOGY

Born in Calcutta, 18th July, 1811.
Charterhouse, 1822.
Trinity College, Cambridge, 1829.
Newspaper ventures and art studies, 1833–5.
Marriage, 1836.
Fraser's, 1837.
Birth of Anne Thackeray, 1837.
Yellowplush Papers, 1838.
Birth of Harriet Marian Thackeray, 1840.
Paris Sketch Book published, 1840.
Wife's insanity, 1840.
Joins *Punch*, 1842.
Barry Lyndon, 1844.
Snob Papers in *Punch*, 1846–7.
Vanity Fair, 1847–8.
Pendennis begun, 1848.
Illness, 1849.
Pendennis finished, 1850.
Lecture, *English Humourists*, at Willis' Rooms, 1851.
Esmond, 1851–2.
First American tour, 1852–3.
The Newcomes, 1853–5.
Four Georges and second American tour, 1855–6.
The Virginians, 1857–9.
Editor of *Cornhill Magazine*, 1860.
Lovel the Widower, 1860.
The Roundabout Papers, 1860–2.
Philip, 1860–2.
Resigns from *Cornhill*, 1862.
Denis Duval started, 1863.
Death, 1863.

" Should we be any better than our neighbours? No, certainly. And as we can't be virtuous let us be decent. Fig leaves are a very decent, becoming wear, and have been now in fashion for four thousand years. . . .

" And such (excuse my sermonising) – such is the constitution of mankind that men have, as it were, entered into a compact among themselves to pursue the fig-leaf system à outrance, *and to cry down all who oppose it. Humbug they will have. Humbugs themselves, they will respect humbugs. Their daily victuals of life must be seasoned with humbug. Certain things are there in the world that they will not allow to be called by their right names and will insist upon our admiring, whether we will or no. . . ."*

MICHAEL ANGELO TITMARSH.

CHAPTER I

Ancestry – parentage – birth – school – university – Dr. Maginn and Bohemia – inheritance.

THE ancestry of the author of *The Book of Snobs* was important. Fortunately it was also satisfactory. But though the Thackerays were good Yorkshire yeoman stock, such fame as was theirs before the birth of William Makepeace was gained, not in England, but in India.

The novelist's great-grandfather had indeed become Headmaster of Harrow and Chaplain to the Prince of Wales, and an earlier ancestor had gained less worldly honours in the fires of Smithfield, but it was in India, as a servant of the great "John Company," that Thackeray's grandfather began in 1766 that honourable tradition of Indian service that helped to consolidate both British rule and the family fortunes.

The pioneer had a brief but distinguished career. He not only reduced to order the turbulent province of Sylhet, leaving a building known as Thackeray House as an inspiration to his successors, but traded so successfully on his own account that, at the age of twenty-seven, he was able to retire with a wife to England, and support with a comfortable income the rôle of a county squire.

Of his sons, six went to India, five dying either

of the climate or in tribal warfare and one of journalism and drink, but none making the fortune his father had made.

Richmond Thackeray, the second son, did for Birbhum what his father had done for Sylhet; was rewarded with an important post in "the Company's" service at Calcutta; and married in 1810, Anne Becher, aged seventeen and the leading beauty in Calcutta society. But he died five years later, leaving his widow with a son who had been born on the 18th July, 1811, and duly christened William Makepeace.

Four year old when his father died, the future satirist remained with his mother two more years before being put on a ship for England. The voyage via the Cape led to a call at St. Helena, where the boy who was to find his literary inspiration in the eighteenth century saw the exiled executioner of that elegant age, in the person of the captive Napoleon, who, according to the black servant accompanying the little English boy, was still satisfying his strange craving for a daily diet of sheep and children.

In England, the lonely child was received by a trio of elderly ladies in successive stages of seniority. There was his father's sister, Aunt Ritchie, who lived in London; his mother's aunt, Great-aunt Becher, and his mother's grandmother, Great-grandmamma Becher. With the last two he went to live at Fareham, where the society was "mainly composed of wives, widows and daughters of His Majesty's Navy."

In later years he says of Fareham, which has become Fairport in *Denis Duval* :

"There were scarcely any men in Fairport society. There were many widows and elderly spinsters. It was certainly not an intellectual society."

But he gives a rather charming picture of Great-grandmamma Becher (Madam Duval), in " sleeves ruffled at the elbows and mittens of black lace." She walked " on the prettiest little high-heeled shoes bearing a tortoise-shell cane before her. . . . She carried a snuff-box and a tooth-pick and used both with perfect grace."

It is a charming picture when seen with all the enchantment of distance, but probably in experience rather trying. A great-grandmother and a great-aunt, and the relicts of dead sea-captains, with tea at six, a quadrille, and whist till eleven, must have left a lot of room for vagrant thoughts in the creator of the roystering, duelling, dicing, wife-beating Barry Lyndon.

To Aunt Ritchie belongs the credit of discovering the first sign of genius in her nephew. The boy's head fitted his uncle's hat ! But as Uncle Ritchie had never given any signs of genius, Aunt Ritchie regarded the adult skull of her little nephew with more alarm than anticipation. A doctor was summoned. Indulgently he patted the too massive head and shook his own with a reassuring smile :

" He has a large head, but there is a great deal in it."

It was the turning-point in the boy's life.

Henceforth careful note was to be made of all those little evidences of greatness in the boyhood of a great man, which are also so frequently found in the boyhood of men who never become great.

He was sent from his great-grandmother's house to school in Hampshire, but was so unhappy that he was removed and placed at another in Chiswick, where he was treated more humanely. From Chiswick he went to Charterhouse, not at that time situated among the pines and gorse of Surrey, but standing among the smuts of Smithfield. Though later he paid the traditional tribute of affection to " the old school," his emotions during his sojourn there are best described in his own language :

" I was licked into indolence, abused into sulkiness and bullied into despair."

Bad eyesight prevented his taking any part in games, and a stern headmaster any interest in his studies. But he began to cause confusion in the minds of those who were eagerly watching for signs that should support the promise of so large a head. He began to do sketches, to the horror of Martin Tupper – a monitor – and to do them of his masters and on the leaves of his school-books ! But the family were not alarmed. He was obviously going to be an artist. And then he helped to foster a scheme for a school magazine which, though it never came to life, had a poem already written for it by Thackeray. It was a parody of one by " L. E. L.," a well-known though anonymous Sappho, whose treacly muse was much in vogue with the neo-Byronists. This looked as though after all, he was not going to be an artist but a writer. Unfortunately, Thackeray himself was many years learning which of his two talents was the more valuable. At the time of their simultaneous emergence he seems to have been doing nothing more ambitious than to amuse himself in the intervals of being " bullied into despair." He was, however, reading Scott and novels of Corinthian life in London, and a while later, when his mother returned to England with a new husband, had evidently to control his tastes in this direction, for he writes :

" I have not read any novel this term, except one by the author of *Granby*."

Thackeray was happy both in his mother and in his step-father. The latter he shows us in Colonel Newcome, but his real name was Captain H. Carmichael Smythe, retired Indian Army, later awarded the retiring rank of major. The old soldier early removed to Larkbeare, to live the life of a squire, while his wife supported the rôle by driving in a carriage with a footman on the box. It was the schoolboy's first intimate view of Mr. Yellowplush.

At school he was now dabbling in story-writing, but nothing remains of these early efforts and he left Charterhouse for Cambridge carrying with him no distinctions save a nose broken in a fight with a school friend.

The Major accompanied him to Alma Mater, inspected his rooms, chatted with the dons, tipped him, sighed, and departed. But Aunt

Ritchie had given him a letter of introduction to a small outpost of Thackerays not far from the town, where, among other attractions, was the society of a lady of whom little is known but her age – which was ninety.

They could do no more for the boy, except pray for him. And that they soon needed to do. For, once the Major and Aunt Ritchie had turned their backs, William began to sow his wild oats.

It is the most difficult period of Thackeray's life, from the point of view of the biographer. For there are two sources of his life-story ; one, his own novels, which are admittedly autobiographical, and the other, a casket jealously guarded by the family. This casket owes its origin to Thackeray himself, who, towards the end of his life, had been reading a biography of Thomas Hood by the dead poet's son and daughter. Nauseated by the mixture of sentimentality, pomposity and tendenciously selected facts, he shut the book with a bang and said : " Let there be nothing of this when I am gone." Vain hope ! The obedient reverence of his family left his memory for nearly half a century at the mercy of his detractors, only to prompt an attempt at tardy salvage by methods hardly less dangerous to the dead man's reputation. For, between detractors, relations and friends, the luckless giant emerges from the grave, Janus-headed, with one face showing a cynical sneer and the other a saintly smile.

In 1898 a complete edition of his works was published by Smith Elder, to which his daughter, the late Lady Ritchie, contributed a biographical introduction, illustrated at intervals by selected passages from selected letters, mostly to his mother. It was these letters of which Thackeray said, when speaking of Steerforth's letter to his mother in *David Copperfield*:

"My letters to my mother are like this, but then she likes 'em – like Mrs. Steerforth."

This rather detracts from their value as evidence, and perhaps from our good opinion of Thackeray himself. But what was he to do? Fond of his mother as he was, he was a young man when he first obeyed her injunction to tell her everything in his letters, and young men usually find that there are some things they cannot tell even their mothers. But he told his public later, in two books, *Pendennis* and *Lovel the Widower*, and to them we must turn for a picture of his life at Cambridge and for the reason why he left the university at the end of a year and without a degree.

For only a reason can be given. Excuse there was none, since he was immediately placed in the society of such subsequently famous company as Frederick and Alfred Tennyson, Monckton Milnes (afterwards Lord Houghton), Edward Fitzgerald, W. H. Brookfield and Venables (who was to become famous as the boy who broke the nose of the most famous novelist of the day). That Thackeray knew all these men is true, but with only one of them was he ever really intimately friendly. Venables and Brookfield he saw much of in later life, but of Alfred Tennyson, little ; and, at Cambridge, Tennyson could hardly have been very friendly with him, since Thackeray parodied in the university magazine, *The Snob*, Alfred's prize poem, "Timbuctoo."

In Fitzgerald alone did Thackeray find a man after his own heart. Gruff, loyal old Fitz fled too from his age, as Thackeray did, but not with Thackeray to the eighteenth century. Fitz went further in time and place, to the "wilderness" of the old Persian tent-maker, Omar Khayyám. Always ready to help when asked, and often when not asked, by the rather forgetful Thackeray, Fitzgerald was a strange anomalous character, who lived with old sailors on his little yacht; a lonely, rather lovable figure, singing softly to himself of "bowls of wine" and "books of verse" and the "sorry scheme of things entire," while all about him the bright and busy century was removing the wigs from the heads of the wits and clapping them on to the skulls of their flunkeys.

With such a man, Thackeray spent some time and read some books, learned Greek and found his literary hero, Fielding. But he also met a man his mother did not approve, one Carne, the prototype of Bloundell-Bloundell, in *Pendennis*.

With Bloundell-Bloundell he learned to hold his wine and lose his money, to follow the hounds and, perhaps, to ogle. The lid of the casket opens, and out peeps a letter to his mother. It is about the parody on Tennyson's prize poem, "Timbuctoo":

"'Timbuctoo' received much laud. I could

not help finding that I was very fond of this same praise. The men know not the author, but praise the poem : how eagerly I sucked it in ! ' All is vanity ! ' "

It is a reassuring letter. At twenty, the youth who was to become famous as the author of *Vanity Fair* has struck the right note with " All is vanity." If, however, we turn to *Pendennis* or *Lovel the Widower*, we cannot entirely dismiss the possibility that this early cry from the disciple of Ecclesiastes may have been the result of indisposition following a night prolonged in the rooms of Bloundell-Bloundell. Perhaps with such conflicting evidence it is best to let Thackeray speak of himself, as gruff old Fitz averred he was too fond of doing in his novels :

" Perhaps," he says in *Lovel the Widower*, " I read too many novels, occupied myself too much with ' elegant literature ' and spoke too often at the Union. . . . But those fine words got me no college prizes : I missed my fellowship ; was rather in disgrace with my relations afterwards."

And suddenly, with no clear explanation either from the family or himself, he crosses to the Continent, to begin his first real experience of a society that always suited him better than that to be found in his genteel England.

" There are a hundred good reasons," he wrote, later in life, to his mother, " for a lazy, liberal, extravagant but not costly way of life." He found some at Weimar, where he was caught by the wings and settled joyfully to taste the flavour of the society he later limned in the Pumpernickel of

Vanity Fair. It was a setting after his own heart. Pretty women, a Grand Duke and the picturesque punçtilio of a petty Court, a meeting with Goethe, heart-free love for the Princess, culminated in a longing for a cornetcy in a yeomanry regiment, so that he could mingle with the other uniformed gallants without " looking something like a cross between a footman and a Methodist."

Indulging the " lazy, liberal, extravagant but not costly way of life," he fluttered his wings in Weimar for some months, till he tasted one of his periodic attacks of self-mistrust and uneasiness. He saw his contemporaries at Cambridge settling down to dignified drudgery of one sort or another, and experienced a sudden panic that he might find no drudgery to dignify him. In a letter to his mother he writes as a Harry turning his back upon a Falstaff to pick up the sceptre and become King. The throne he chose was a lawyer's stool at No. 1, Hare Court, Temple, whereon he seated himself to read the law with a Mr. Taprell.

But his good resolution soon wilted in the dust of the law, despite his attempt to relieve the monotony by a good deal of town gaiety, including a theatre at least once a week, and the greater delight of the pantomime. He also managed to visit Cambridge, where he met old friends, and to accept London invitations, where he made new ones. A favourite haunt of his, the Bedford, was the scene of more than one convivial evening, while as leaven he might claim a meeting with John Stuart Mill.

He was already reading " Christopher North "

in *Blackwood's,* and probably developing that taste for cut-and-thrust reviewing which later, under the fostering care of that doyen of literary brigands, Dr. Maginn, developed into the joyous invective of his contributions to *Fraser's Magazine.*

Exactly when he began to see less of Hare Court and more of Grub Street cannot definitely be stated, but his sponsor in the rather disreputable literary Bohemia he was soon to enter was an Irish Jesuit, one Father Mahoney. This bright-eyed, scholarly little rascal, with a store of ribald stories and an unslakable thirst, had earlier found that his convictions clashed with his conviviality, and, recklessly bartering his anticipation of happiness in the next world for the certainty of enjoyment in this, plunged into journalism under the sobriquet of " Prout," retaining only the title of " Father " to indicate, among much evidence of the weakness of the flesh, a still-surviving willingness of the spirit.

It was he who introduced Thackeray to " bright, broken Maginn " – scholar, novelist, wit and drunkard. At the time of the introduction, Maginn was still " bright " and not yet " broken." An Irishman of quite unusual versatility, he had passed brilliantly through Dublin University, obtaining the degree of Doctor of Law at the age of twenty-three ; had taught in his father's school, and on his father's death had made both himself and his school famous ; had begun to use his pen, attracted the notice of *Blackwood's* and contributed to that journal ; was the author of a clever satirical novel, *Whitehall, or the Days of George IV*, in which the Duke of Wellington was caricatured ; had forsaken his school for free-lance journalism ; was the friend of Lockhart and of Barnes, a contributor to the *Literary Gazette* and the *Quarterly* and was then editing *Fraser's*, which already equalled in brilliance and surpassed in scurrility the not over-delicate *Blackwood's*. The doctor was also associated with the rather shady Theodore Hook, and an occasional contributor to *John Bull*, a paper that thrived by washing soiled but costly linen in public. He later sank lower, to join Westmacott and the *Age*, which set up as a rival laundry to *John Bull* and improved on its contemporary's technique by a system which permitted, for a consideration, the removal of the clothes from the line. Yet Maginn was a good friend and a staunch enemy ; could borrow money as readily as he would lend his wit ; had as keen an eye for a pretty woman as he had sharp an ear for literary quackery ; could detect and encourage talent as readily as he would lampoon a fool ; and withal could forget both women and friends, fools and debts, in pursuit of the only lasting passion he ever knew – gin. He exercised in his day a greater influence than can be fully measured on men whose names are remembered by those who have never heard of his ; was unflinchingly loyal to intellect when he met it ; and helped many to the success he missed himself while drifting dizzily down Grub Street, pen in one hand and bottle in the other, to the Fleet Prison and consumption, which led to his release both from gaolers and life at the early age of forty-eight.

To Thackeray he was undoubtedly a friend, for he borrowed his money and encouraged his talent. Thackeray himself was captivated by the wit and scholarship of his mentor, and wrote enthusiastically of a morning spent listening to the " Doctor " reading Homer in a " manner that gave to it a new meaning." He also accompanied him into the haunts of literary Bohemia and had his first view of the personalities behind the ranks of bristling pens which were then stabbing savagely at most literary figures in the public eye.

Among such needy but gallant soldiers of fortune the rather dandified figure of young Thackeray must have struck a contrast. In his portrait by Maclise, in 1831, he appears as a very tall and finished young " buck," in long-tailed coat, tight-fitting trousers strapped beneath the boots, a fashionably high collar, big cravat-tie, and a monocle. The plentiful and elegantly disordered hair, and the incipient " moustachios," set off a face chiefly noticeable for one feature, the mouth, almost babyish in shape yet with a faintly aggressive passivity, suggestive of a nature prepared to remain silent unless listened to with more than mere politeness.

In the " Doctor's " society he learned to hold his wine more easily than to digest the law, for, beyond expressing to his step-father a proper contempt for such a profession, he makes no further reference to the career he had chosen.

The more seemly side of his life at this time is revealed by Lady Ritchie :

" In the early years my father spent in London, trying his prentice hand, his circle of friends, E. Fitzgerald, Chas. and Arthur Buller, John and Henry Kemble, Alfred and Frederick Tennyson, used to meet and play and work together, or sit over their brandy and water discussing men and books and morals, speculating, joking and contradicting each other – liking fun and talk and wit and humour, and all fanciful and noble things."

The brandy and water adds a note of verisimilitude, and, for the rest, Thackeray was always a man of catholic tastes. Mildly interested in the Reform Agitation, he also at this time spent a holiday in Cornwall on the nominal excuse of assisting his friend Buller's candidature for Liskeard, and, reading, sketching and dining with friends, he whiled away a pleasant adolescence till he woke, on the 18th July, 1832, to find himself twenty-one years of age and master of his own patrimony.

It was the day he had " been panting for." Without waiting even to tell Mr. Taprell, he abandoned the law for ever and crossed straight from Cornwall to France, where there were a good cuisine, cheap wine, pretty women, and a gentleman or two upon the boulevards, instead of a line of footmen behind the area railings.

CHAPTER II

" Wild oats " – newspaper ventures – the last of the patrimony – Fraser's Magazine – Bulwer-baiting – marriage – hack-journalism – Yellowplush and Michael Angelo Titmarsh – wife's insanity.

WE have Trollope's authority for placing Thackeray's patrimony at a figure which yielded some five hundred a year – a capital sum that seems roughly adequate to the calls he made on it before it finally vanished.

He was determined, he assured his mother, to take from his riches " a regular monthly income which I will never exceed." But he gave no indication of a choice of career to add to his determination. He was going to study history, philosophy and other serious works, like his friend, Fitzgerald. But Maginn had hinted that a literary career was not beneath the attention of a gentleman, and Thackeray made a note of the idea. Settled in Paris, he pursued his studies, enlarging both his mind and his circle of friends. *The Paris Sketch Book*, published some years later, shows him to have applied himself assiduously to both books and life. Only a man who had really read history could have written much that is to be found in it, and only one who had not cared much what company he kept could have produced some of the seamy, often sinister, little vignettes that make the book so rich a part of Thackeray's work.

It was a strange world he had been born into. Railways and telegraph had not yet arrived to compress it into a consistent whole. There were queer little backwaters of eighteenth-century corruption without eighteenth-century elegance. The aristocrat still shone in Pumpernickel, while the liveried flunkey dazzled Tyburnia. England was becoming middle class, while the Continent still held to the shreds of a less respectable régime. A voyage from Dover to Boulogne could take a man out of one century into another, and many out of reach of the debtors' prison into the haven of a seamy, flashy but glittering world of demi-beaumondaines and demi-reps. The Continental watering-place and spa were the debtor's sanctuary. Here came the colonels without regiments, the Altamonts and Costigans, the spendthrift heirs of the Lords Cinqbars and Bareacres; slippery, seamy flotsam, fleeing from the sponging-house, the Fleet and Marshalsea, to hover round the cafés and the gaming-tables in wait for elegant young "pigeons" with feathers all puffed out, ready for plucking.

And among the season's birds was Thackeray, to whom bowed the Hon. Deuceace, before suggesting écarté, at which he speedily relieved him of a good part of his patrimony.

Thackeray seems to have lost with the eighteen-century grace he so frequently describes in his studies of that age, and in after years pointed out to a friend a seedy-looking gentleman at Spa, with the comment:

"I have not seen that man since he drove me

down in his cabriolet to my bankers in the city, where I sold out my patrimony and paid it over to him."

Such a statement suggests either that his memory was at fault or, as is more likely, that he exaggerated with the unconscious artistry of middle age the since-redeemed follies of youth, for there was enough good money left to throw after bad, in an attempt to run a literary paper.

The failure of an Indian bank had in the meantime sufficiently reduced the step-father's income to induce that rather sanguine soldier to join his step-son in an endeavour to re-establish their joint fortunes. The Major and his step-son therefore acquired an interest in the *National Standard and Journal of Literature, Science, Music, Theatricals and the Fine Arts,* founded by one F. W. N. Bayley, who was also editing it in the intervals of drinking himself to death.

A creature from the Grub Street gutters, Bayley had served as one of Theodore Hook's scavengers on the staff of *John Bull*, and was now affecting, both in his writings and his speech, the style of Dr. Maginn. The only real resemblance he had no need to simulate – it had already been acquired, and led him, as it did his exemplar, to an early death.

With such an editor, it is not perhaps surprising that among the earlier editorial announcements was one that the editor had left – with how much cash in the form of a solatium, we do not know. Still, he had done his work well, and, by the time he left, it could not be undone. First published in

January, the *National Standard* lasted till the following December, when it died and was reborn as the *Literary Standard*, with the price increased to threepence, only to die again, this time fatally, in February 1834.

Thackeray himself bestowed upon its fortunes very little more energy and enterprise than he had on the law. But he had himself appointed Paris correspondent, which enabled him to combine profit with pleasure, and sent a weekly letter regularly for a while, after which he lost interest or, more truly, discovered a new one.

To his mother he writes :

" I have been thinking very seriously of becoming an artist ; I think I can draw better than I can do anything else."

Up to the time fo writing, that was true enough, and in any case he was probably attracted more by the status and life of an artist in Paris than by the rather disreputable rank and toil of a journalist in London. In *The Paris Sketch Book* he shows a keen understanding of the difference between the French and English attitude to both art and letters.

In the meantime, the *atelier* was certainly a very delightful rendezvous and the artist an even more delightful companion.

" Yesterday," he writes, " we had a breakfast for five consisting of five sausages, three loaves, and a bottle of wine for fifteen sous. Afterwards pipes, then songs succeeded."

The hour at which painting succeeded is not stated. But despite the cheapness of the breakfasts, when he returned to England to face the imminent collapse of the *National Standard* his artist friends had left him little more than the price of its obsequies.

But he writes to his mother, thanking heaven for making him poor, which, he adds, has made him much happier. What his mother thought of his new-found happiness we can only guess, for he adds:

"I shall now have to palm myself off on you and father, just at the time when I ought to be independent."

At this crisis, Maginn reappeared and Thackeray began his real journalistic career with articles published pseudonymously in *Fraser's Magazine for Town and County*. Still flitting between Paris and London, he still betrayed a greater faith in himself as an artist than as a writer, for the first of his books published was *Flore et Zephyr*, a collection of his drawings, with no letterpress. They needed none. It is curious that among his many friends there was none who, having seen his drawing, encouraged him to persevere in his writing. He himself had always admired Hogarth. But Hogarth's virile coarseness had never been emasculated by prudery. And Thackeray's was. Apart from the fact that Hogarth was an artist and Thackeray never more than an illustrator, the nineteenth-century imitator of the eighteenth-century master produced a combination of coarseness and facetiousness that reached an extraordinarily high level of vulgarity.

But *Flore et Zephyr* was not yet published, and

Fraser's Magazine was his stand-by, as Maginn and Mahoney were his mentors in that always savage, frequently caddish and sometimes brilliant type of reviewing which distinguished the first few decades of the nineteenth century. *Blackwood's* and the *Quarterly* had initiated it, and specimens of both these papers' treatment of Keats' *Endymion* may confirm the reputation for virulence without revealing that quality of brilliance with which contemporary opinion credited them.

The *Quarterly* accused Keats of copying Leigh Hunt and " found the poem so tedious as to be unreadable," adding that its chief quality was " calm, settled, imperturbable, drivelling idiocy."

Blackwood's, in an attempt to paint the *Quarterly's* lily, added a personal reference to Keats' having qualified as a surgeon, with the injunction: " Back to the shop, Mr. John, stick to plasters, pills, ointment boxes."

Fortunately, Keats was dead, for he had shown signs of proving the critics to be wrong. There was no such risk with their new butt, Bulwer, as yet without the baronetcy and " Lytton," but with all the other qualities that endeared him to Maginn and his followers as the " gameness " of a fox endears him to the huntsman and his hounds.

There was some justification for their whips and scorpions, for even Tennyson called him " the padded man who wears the stays." Though he outlived his preposterous posing, Bulwer at this time was a figure of almost unbelievable absurdity. And yet, though the most popular butt of the critics, he was the most popular novelist of the public.

He inherited a double tradition and catered for a dual taste. Byron had set the vogue of the melancholy and disillusioned idealist, made cynical by fate ; Mrs. Radcliffe had made popular the " gothic " novel, in which moonlight and ruins were the setting, and tempests and groans the accompaniment of her impassioned lovers, clasping each other to their buckram breasts. Bulwer embraced the dual destiny. He had already actually acted in a personal drama of the " gothic " type. He had spent one whole moonlit (but warm) night lying upon the grave of his dead lady-love. Arising, cramped but otherwise unharmed, he turned and faced the world – in Byron's collar, his wife's stays and Mrs. Radcliffe's moonlight.

But fickle fashion changed. The " fashionable " novel became the vogue. It dealt with high life, the drawing-room, the carriage, the flunkey, and the prayer-book on the satin cushion. This class of novel was called " silver fork " fiction, and Bulwer, with an uncanny faculty for detecting a coming change in public taste, changed his wares quickly and set about busily " polishing silver forks."

The new *genre* proved as popular as the old. Taking off their coats, Maginn and his merry men set about their " padded " dandy in earnest.

Those were strenuous days. The eighteenth century was dead at last, leaving behind it only a few pale shadows of its elegants. Industrialism

and war services had provided a new peerage, a
" factoristocracy," who, not quite sure how their
coronets and robes should be worn, rushed
feverishly to Bulwer's novels to learn. It was the
golden age of " *arrivisme*," when society was
divided between those who had been born great,
those who had achieved greatness, and a fever-
ish number rushing hither and thither in their
efforts to have greatness thrust upon them.
Between " tuft-hunters " and the already tufted
was a fierce but fragile friendship, while in the
background a truculent and often scurrilous army
of journalists, with powers bigger than their
incomes, animated by violent political prejudices
and smarting under a struggling penury on the
fringe of parvenu Tyburnia, watched eagerly for
and seized savagely upon any evidence of the
" snobbery " which Thackeray later was to make
his private heresy hunt.

In truth the wheel had come full circle since
Pope, in the *Dunciad*, had caned the seedy
journalists of his day. The middle class that had
wept over Richardson's *Clarissa*, while Walpole
and the wits raised literature to its most polished
pinnacle, had now moved out of their little houses
into bigger ones, had made money and were
spending it by besieging the circles the wits had
vacated. And Grub Street had profited by the
change. Maginn need not fear to lose his ears
in the pillory as Defoe had done. He had a
public behind him – not the elegant wits of
Pope's circle, but the newly genteel, who were
prodigious readers of books. But, though great

readers, their taste had not kept pace with their fortunes. *Fraser's* public was always just a step behind, mistaking facetiousness for humour, humour for wit, wit for cynicism and abuse for criticism.

Into this new " Battle of the Books " Thackeray plunged with much eagerness, considerable aptitude and few reservations. The method was that used on Keats by the *Quarterly* and *Blackwood's* – the *argumentum ad hominem*. Describe your victim – clothes, appearance and origin, especially if, like Disraeli's, it was Jewish. Then, having aroused in your public a friendly interest in your man, accuse him of " tuft-hunting," " political hypocrisy," " silver fork polishing " ; of everything except artistic incompetence or literary insincerity. That came last, in the peroration, which sank to silence to the words of a kind of literary *Nunc dimittis*.

Bulwer, already a St. Sebastian bristling with Grub Street arrows, now received the attentions of a new archer. And Thackeray's shafts nearly put him out of his agony. Thackeray has been accused of jealousy in the matter, and in certain aspects jealousy it was. But not jealousy of Bulwer's work. Between the author of *Godolphin* and the author of *Vanity Fair* was the same gulf that divided Fielding from Richardson. One was the protagonist of the novel of sentiment, the other of the novel of manners. Bulwer was also a poseur and a coxcomb, and Thackeray's conception of a snob was wider than the public's. It embraced every man who claimed to be what he was not – whether a baronet or a genius. And at that time Bulwer was neither, and, indeed, never became anything but the first. Moreover, Bulwer could change his clothes so adroitly. When later the new craze for criminals produced the fiction known as " Newgate novels," Bulwer left his " ruins " and " silver forks " and produced his *Paul Clifford* and *Eugene Aram*. And Thackeray, shifting his ground, attacked the new sham and, not only scarified the romanticism of the " baronet " in always making his highwaymen and thieves tender and gallant gentlemen, but wrote himself *The Luck of Barry Lyndon*, which showed the real scoundrel and his century in such a brilliant light as lit up the whole interior of the tinsel booth in which Bulwer's buckram highwaymen pirouetted genteelly before their genteel public.

Moreover, Bulwer was not Thackeray's only prey. Later, in *Punch Prize Novelists*, he took him again, but only to head the noble procession which included Disraeli, G. P. R. James, Charles Lever and Harrison Ainsworth. Indeed, Thackeray's letter in later life to Lady Blessington, though it has been stated to be an effort to gain an entrée to Gore House by sycophancy, contains so eminently sane a reason for his dislike of Bulwer's work as should convince most people that it was the style, not the man, he disliked.

" There are sentiments in his [Bulwer's] writings," he says, " which always anger me, big words which make me furious, and a premeditated fine writing against which I can't help rebelling."

In short he, as did most of his contemporaries, disliked the English which has been called "Bulwerese." As to his jealousy of Bulwer, it was twofold. Bulwer moved in the world out of which Thackeray had been driven in the cabriolet of the Hon. Deuceace, and Bulwer was making a fortune out of the scented rhodomontade which Thackeray had to review for a pittance.

But, if he was entitled to his literary victims, the *ad hominem* method of attacking them is less easily justifiable. The extenuation, if not the excuse, was the journalistic standard of the day. *Fraser's* and *Blackwood's* were near enough to the eighteenth century to feel some of its influence. And the *Dunciad* had been hard-hitting. Unfortunately, Maginn was no Pope, nor Mahoney a Swift. Instead of vitriol they threw mud, and, though it did not sear, it stuck. It also dirtied the hand that threw it more than the face it hit. It was many years before Thackeray could wash his hands of that earlier essay in mud-larking, and by that time he had received a good deal of mud in his own face.

But *Fraser's* was more than a literary midden. Among the contributors was Carlyle, and in Maclise's famous sketch of "The Fraserians" the youthful Thackeray sits at the round table and surveys through his monocle a company that included Coleridge, then in an honourable dotage, Barry Cornwall and Harrison Ainsworth, a handsome young buck, famous as the author of *Rookwood*.

Still, on the whole, Thackeray was enjoying

Cт

himself, dividing his time between *Fraser's* in London and the Louvre in Paris. But there was a fly in the Parisian ointment, for in Paris was another member of the female hierarchy which watched over his wayward ways. His maternal grandmother gave him shelter and advice in Paris, whither she had moved for economy's sake. After a boyhood with Great-grandmamma Becher, Thackeray was faced with a Parisian manhood with Grandmamma Butler.

But he was a young man of spirit, and, after a preliminary course of hints that he would work better in rooms of his own, he got them in the Rue des Beaux Arts and entered them with the vow to " work hard and lead a most pious, sober and godly life."

He began well, by falling in love with a girl whom his friend, Reeve, describes as " a nice, simple, girlish girl." Thackeray had met her at the house of Eyre E. Crowe, Paris correspondent of the *Morning Chronicle*. There is anominous family silence about Thackeray's *fiancée*, though Lady Ritchie states that her father once told her he fell in love with her mother's voice. All that is known of this rather mysterious and wholly tragic girl is that she had as father one of those too numerous " colonels " who lived on the Continent for the sake of " economy," and for mother a woman who became, in Thackeray's eyes, the veritable principle of female evil. She was Irish and, like all Irish people, of " good family." She had a " foul, loud tongue, a stupid head, a bad temper, an immense pride and arrogance, an extravagant son and very little money."

It is the friend of Lovel the Widower speaking, but it is Thackeray's voice and his last debt discharged to the sponging harridan who appears first as the Campaigner in *The Newcomes*, and last as Lady Baker in *Lovel the Widower*. Bad as she was as the Campaigner, she is revolting as Lady Baker. It is the same voice speaking about her " angel child," the same bragging Irish tongue that threw in the face of Thackeray's mother (Mrs. Bonnington) her poverty and lack of experience of the *beau monde* that had fluttered round the viceregal Court in Dublin in the Campaigner's palmy days. And the bitter, vindictive but pitiful voice of Thackeray, nearing his grave, rings back across his life to these days :

" And so, when a white-armed siren was bedevilling *me* with her all too tempting ogling and singing, I did not see at the time, but *now* I know that her artful mother was egging that artful child on."

What the Thackeray family thought of the engagement we do not know. There is no letter quoted at this critical time. They probably hoped for the best, for Rose Newcome, away from the Campaigner had a few qualities of her own. Meanwhile, Thackeray had nothing to marry on but his earnings, which were small, and a promise of fifty pounds per annum from the Campaigner, for " pin money " for her angel. Re-establishing his almost lapsed connection with *Fraser's*, he tried to obtain the post of illustrator to the *Pickwick Papers*, the work of a young journalist, known as " Boz." He gained a personal interview with Dickens, but the sketches were rejected as unsuitable, and, unable to wait for his fame as an artist to relieve his penury as a lover, he applied to his step-father for the means to marry.

Once again the gallant old soldier took the field, and, being unable to increase his step-son's allowance, decided to make money by a fresh venture into the realms where he had already lost some. In 1836, Major Carmichael Smythe emerged from obscurity as chairman of the Metropolitan Newspaper Company, with a capital of £60,000 and the ownership of a moribund newspaper, the *Public Ledger*. Re-christened the *Constitutional and Public Ledger*, the first number was published in September 1836, with Blanchard as editor, Douglas Jerrold as dramatic critic, and Thackeray as Paris correspondent at a salary of £400 per annum.

Thus assured financially for as long as the paper lasted (which was nine months), Thackeray married. But, as he said himself in after years :

" I would do it again, for behold love is the crown and completion of all earthly good," adding, less transcendentally, " The man who is afraid of his fortune never deserved one."

The *Constitutional and Public Ledger* was a newspaper of radical views and good tone, and failed because of both. Unwilling to compete in scurrility with the popular *Age*, *John Bull*, and other disreputable organs, it was unable to impress its radicalism upon the genteel.

Thackeray was the first retrenchment, a Paris correspondent being too expensive a luxury for a languishing journal. He thus early saw the impending doom of the paper, its chairman and himself, and tried feverishly to obtain other work. An offer of more sketches, this time to Harrison Ainsworth for his novel *Crichton*, was no more successful than with Dickens. And then the *Constitutional* failed.

The sanguine old soldier was virtually ruined, and retired to Paris, leaving his step-son to arrange the liquidation of his debts. For the first time in his life, Thackeray had to face realities, and to his credit it must be said that he did so manfully. Colonel Newcome himself was not more honourable than Major Carmichael Smythe in his determination to meet all liabilities ultimately. But it was left to Thackeray's pen to defend his step-father's honour, and it was not till 1848, when he was famous as the author of *Vanity Fair*, that he discharged the old man's last liability and reaped the last crop of his own " wild oats."

In the previous June his first child had been born, and when he had settled his parents in Paris it was to No. 13, Great Coram Street that he went with his wife and small daughter to begin writing for a living.

It was now that some of the crop of friends who had grown up among his oats helped him – the Stirlings, to an occasional article or review for *The Times*, and loyal Fitzgerald with small commissions for illustrating, and a great tongue that praised him and bothered all and sundry to help him.

For *The Times* he reviewed Carlyle's *French Revolution*, and thereby almost pleased the Diogenes of letters, for in a letter on the subject the latter described Thackeray, picturesquely if inaccurately, as " a half-monstrous Cornish giant, kind of painter, Cambridge man and Paris newspaper correspondent," adding with strict veracity, " who is now writing for his life in London."

Of Thackeray's married life we know little. It began dismally enough, financially. Article-writing and a little reviewing, a short story for *Bentley's Miscellany*, then edited by Dickens, and *The Great Hogarty Diamond*, which was refused by *Blackwood's*, make up a meagre measure of success from the pen which he still believed was only an auxiliary to the artist's brush. But Theodore Hook smelt promise in the man who had written for *Bentley's* under the pseudonym of " Goliath Gahagan," and filched him from his less astute rival to contribute to the *New Monthly* and, later, to the *Examiner*.

The ephemeral nature of most of his work gives little evidence on which to estimate his real situation at this time, and we can only guess by the number of periodicals he wrote for, that none had learned to value his contributions at more than standard rates. A little money for illustrating came his way, but the illustrations were not to the taste of the critics.

He was certainly working very hard, for Fitzgerald refers to him as " writing hard for half a dozen reviews and newspapers all the morning." He was also apparently living fairly hard too, for Fitzgerald continues that he was " dining, drinking and talking of a night . . . under a wear-and-tear of thinking and feeding that would have knocked up any other man I know two years ago, at least."

Of his wife we see and hear little. There is a letter from him written in the first few months of marriage in which he says that he has grown " strangely fat and am the happiest man in the neighbourhood," but most married men begin by being happy, even if they defer becoming fat till later.

At the end of two years, he told his wife that " they had not had a single unhappy day," but on another occasion he also told her that " happiness is as good as prayers." Despite the suitability of the subject, the family letters touch little upon these days, and if we turn to *Lovel the Widower* we are told that " the defunct Cecilia " did not like Lovel's bachelor friends, particularly one who resembles Fitzgerald, and who could be gruff and outspoken. But she sang, and played the harp, the harp which Lovel's friend describes as resting after her death " in a skin of Cordovan leather," " the ghostly musical instrument " about which " I used to leave a sort of *crawly* sensation, as of a sickly genteel ghost flitting about the place in an exceedingly peevish humour trying to scold and command."

The only glimpse we catch of her is in a letter to Thackeray's mother, which is mincing and timid, a combination which does not inspire us with confidence in her ability to comfort and help her struggling, many-sided husband, in his efforts to establish himself as a big figure in a world of big figures. Indeed, it is probable that the tragedy which so soon overtook her prevented another, implicit in their incompatibility, as it also saved her from criticism, by arousing pity. Certain it is that when his second child died he wrote to his mother : " I don't feel sorrow for her, and think of her only as something charming that for a season we were allowed to enjoy . . . but I would not ask to have the child back again and subject her to the degradation of life and pain." This was written after " The Yellowplush Papers " had been published and when life had become a good deal easier financially, yet it suggests experiences more painful than poverty to a man who was by nature convivial and by temper full of good spirits and good courage. But, whatever Thackeray's home life, Mr. Charles Yellowplush was born in 1837 and made his bow to the public in *Fraser's*. The public bowed in return, but a little bewilderedly. For Mr. Yellowplush, despite the delight of his dropped aitches, was rather a cynical fellow for a footman. And the reason was that he was more than a footman. He was a symbol – the avatar of an age of " foot-manners." His plush breeches had hitherto set the cachet on the family whose grandfather's had been of fustian. Now he was wearing them on his own account, and, despite the fact that he was merely a flunkey, he was no fool.˙ He had studied his betters and mastered their technique. Moreover, he was ambitious and aspired to rise above the level of a footman. Could it be that this mute, bewigged automaton had watched his master too closely? It was impossible. It was just a piece of *Fraserian* impertinence, the work of some impudent young journalist who pretended to see in the servility of the flunkey the sycophancy of the master, and to suggest that the wig the footman wished to remove was the same symbol as the coronet his master wished to put on. Fortunately, the footman still dropped his aitches, so they laughed – except a few who began to ask the real name of Mr. Charles Yellowplush.

The Yellowplush Papers were followed by *Strictures on Pictures* by one Michael Angelo Titmarsh. And Titmarsh was almost as impertinent as Yellowplush. Fortunately, he only attacked the artist who was, in any case, a pretty low fellow.

Actually, Titmarsh could say many very sensible things on art. He was no artist himself, and he always sniggered at a " nude " and always looked for a story in a picture, though he could appreciate both colour and composition. But he knew sham whenever he met it, and sentimentality too, and he met both when he went to the Royal Academy. Landseer in painting seems to have been as dear to him as Bulwer in writing. Of his " Shepherd Praying at a Cross in the Field," Titmarsh says : " An almost endless flock of sheep lies round the pious master. . . . The numbers and variety of attitude and expression in that flock of sheep quite startle the spectator as he looks at them."

Of another and now forgotten genius, he writes : " The lad's face is effeminate and imbecile, but his velveteen breeches are painted with much vigour and strength."

The reactions of the artists were violent, and Stone expressed the opinion, if not the hope, that Thackeray would end by being horsewhipped. Actually he ended by being sent to Paris by *The Times* to review the Salon of 1838. For, though he could, and sometimes did, indulge in that essentially English trick, the lampooning of the artist, by the critic, for the Philistine, he could also speak with a curiously modern voice of the slavish worship of the classical that was vitiating French art. He could also write, of some of the stuff that English painters thrust before their public : " Let us, in the name of goodness, make a stand somewhere, or the namby-pamby of the world will become unendurable and we shall melt away in a deluge of blubber. This drivelling, hysterical sentimentality – it is surely the critic's duty to grin it down."

He was now earning enough, not only to maintain his own establishment, but to begin to liquidate his step-father's debts. He was also becoming known – but, unfortunately for his personal success, not as Thackeray but as three different people – Mr. Yellowplush, Mr. Titmarsh and Major Goliath Gahagan. But his composite character did not prevent his being elected as

William Makepeace Thackeray to the Stirling and Shakespeare Clubs.

Following his child's death, he began to write *The Great Hogarty Diamond*, but the efforts of a friend to interest *Blackwood's* in the story failed, and it was not finally published till 1841.

He had better luck, but little success, with *Catherine*, which was published, but failed to attract the attention of any but the discerning few. It was designedly against the stream of " Newgate novels " then pouring in a flood from the pens of many, and most profitably from those of Bulwer and Ainsworth. Even Dickens had felt the need of accommodating popular fancy by *Oliver Twist*, with its thieves' kitchen, Bill Sikes and the impossibly romantic creation – Nancy – who had stepped straight out of a genteel parlour to become a burglar's mistress. Ainsworth's *Jack Sheppard* was a phenomenal success, and Thackeray wrote to his mother that " it is acted at *four* theatres and they say that at the Coburg people are waiting about the lobbies selling *Sheppard-bags* – a bag containing a few pick-locks, that is, a screw driver and iron levers."

Into this sanguinary, if sanguine, world *Catherine* was launched, written, as one editor of the novels says, " in imitation of the bombastic fiction of the day," while Lady Ritchie adds that " the story of the wicked Catherine is one of the grimmest of all my father's, but he still, perhaps, retained the prejudice that crime *is* grim." He undoubtedly did ; but the public retained theirs that it was extremely romantic. As later, with

Barry Lyndon, so now in *Catherine*, he stripped to the very bones the romantic figures of thieves and murderers which were making Bulwer's and Ainsworth's fortunes. His reward was complete neglect, though he was able to record that " the judges stand up for me. Carlyle says it is wonderful and many laud it highly." But it could never have succeeded when we remember that even his daughter, Lady Ritchie, could call it " the most cynical of my father's novels."

Shortly after, as though to confirm him in his view that life differed from the pretty pictures his successful contemporaries drew of it, came his wife's illness following the birth of their third child, in May 1840. He took her to Margate, hoping the change of scene might restore her. But it only confirmed his worst suspicions. Her reason had fled.

CHAPTER III

Bachelor life in London – *Paris Sketch Book* – Charles Lever and *Irish Sketch Book* – *Punch* – *From Cornhill to Cairo* – literary quarrels – *The Luck of Barry Lyndon*.

FOR several months, Thackeray nursed his wife personally. He took her to Cork, thinking that the scenes of her childhood might restore the unbalanced mind. When this failed, he took her to Paris to obtain the best medical treatment and advice. He wrote her letters couched in child-language, hoping thus to penetrate into the sluggish child-idiocy that distinguished her mental disorder. While there seemed any chance of her recovery he was always waiting to bring her back to his home and children. All that could be done, in duty, he did ; but she never recovered, though she outlived him by some thirty years. Of his emotional reactions at this time we know next to nothing. There is one letter written to a member of his wife's family eight years later, in which he harks back to the experience. But it is stilted in phraseology and elaborate in sentiment, both of which qualities were probably necessary, considering that the letter would almost certainly be read by the Campaigner. Another letter, to Mrs. Procter, written at the time, is natural in tone, but it expresses less a deep grief than a mood of mental and emòtional lassitude, a stale but almost impersonal depression, as of a man conscious of too many miseries to be more deeply moved by one than by another.

The only person who really knew what Thackeray suffered was Fitzgerald, and he destroyed all the letters on the subject as being too painful to preserve. Yet they contained innumerable sketches by Thackeray which were preserved and given to his daughter. Fitzgerald also visited him a good deal at this time, and in the empty house at Great Coram Street they revived old bachelor memories and enjoyed " great laughing " about the head of a mutual friend, James Spedding.

The family is silent, but biographical tradition suggests that Thackeray emerged from the ordeal with genius turned to cynicism and joyousness into melancholy. As none of the work which has made him famous had then been written, it is interesting to speculate as to what we might have had in place of *Vanity Fair* and *The Book of Snobs*, had his genius not thus been violently wrenched awry. Actually, of course, he had both courage and common sense, and showed no less in this ordeal than did Charles Lamb in the parallel but more intense horror of his sister's homicidal mania, which began by the frenzied killing of her own mother and recurred at intervals throughout the remainder of her brother's patient life with her, without altering one quality in Lamb's character or affecting one change in the gentle, whimsical sanity of his prose. For genius is a hardy growth and, if the brain survives the shock of tragedy, will soon resume its flowering.

What " good old Fitz " destroyed was probably a record, not of passionate grief at a bereavement, but of sheer terror of a similar affliction in the writer. This horror is reflected in *Lovel the Widower*, in tortuous references to Ireland and a possible straight-waistcoat for himself, and later in letters to Mrs. Brookfield, when finding himself forgetting the names and even the incidents in the earlier parts of the still unfinished *Pendennis*, he speaks, with a whimsicality that thinly veils the fear, of a possible state of imbecility in himself.

Lady Ritchie throws a little light on the subject when she refers to her father's journey to Ireland, less than two years later. Quoting Peg of Limavaddy from *The Irish Sketch Book*, she says :

" One can feel the shadows in the poem as well as the sunshine, and the courage and sweetness of the temper which enabled him to write –

> *Came a Cockney bard*
> *Into Derry City,*
> *Weary was his soul,*
> *Shivering and sad he*
> *Bumped along the road*
> *Leads to Limavaddy.*"

Completing the quotation, she adds :

" What a picture of Ireland, and my father's journey there ! ' Weary was his soul, shivering and sad he.' But though he complained for once, I think it was to make a rhyme to ' Limavaddy.' "

And if it was, it was no discredit to him, for he

had done all that could be done for a wife whose life with him is so veiled by family secrecy. With pity for her tragedy, and horror for the nearness of his own mind to the same ruin, the robust, eminently sane man bumps along the road to Limavaddy to write his *Irish Sketch Book* and return to England and to later fame as the trenchant republican radical of *Punch*, the Torquemada of the Snobs and the Master Showman of *Vanity Fair*.

When the last bill had been paid he found himself practically penniless. His step-father could give him no more help. At this time the Major seems to have lost some more money – not in another newspaper, but in another bank. But he and his wife took the children to live with them in Paris, leaving Thackeray, at the age of twenty-nine, to begin again the seemingly hopeless task of making either a name or a living.

When *The Paris Sketch Book* was published in the previous July, he had written to Wilson of the *Anti-Corn Law Circular*, begging for a " puff " " for poor Titmarsh," but, though it came, it brought no success. He had the same experience when, after witnessing, in company with Monckton Milnes, the state funeral of Napoleon, he wrote *The Second Funeral of Napoleon*. Fitzgerald did his best to induce others to buy " Thackeray's little book . . . as each copy sold puts $7\frac{1}{2}d.$ in T.'s pocket."

But beyond a good notice in *The Times* and the approbation of his friends, as brisk and caustic a piece of descriptive writing as Thackeray ever produced earned for him little more than the price of a single article.

He had, beside Fitzgerald, another staunch advertiser in Mrs. Procter, wife of Barry Cornwall. The house of the Procters was in Upper Harley Street, and the poet himself had been the friend of Lamb and Hazlitt, as he was now of Carlyle. Here were to be found most of those who were in any way distinguished in literature and the arts, and here Thackeray found the first of his female friends, and, judged by actual service done to him, the most staunch. She too did her best to popularise *The Second Funeral of Napoleon*, but with no better success than Fitzgerald. But she did succeed in giving Thackeray an outlet for his feelings by giving him the entrée to her home and exchanging letters with him, and later, when *Vanity Fair* hung fire, was one cause of its starting upon the journey to success.

Hack-journalism was still his main means of support, though in the following year he again tried his fortunes by the publications of *Comic Tales and Sketches*, containing all the best of his periodical work, including " Yellowplush " and " Major Gahagan," the whole bearing the name of his third self, Michael Angelo Titmarsh. The sales amounted to 140 copies, and he could only console himself with the remark that " the donkeys of a public don't know a good thing when they get it."

The Great Hogarty Diamond also appeared serially in *Fraser's*, but, despite Stirling's assertion that " there is more truth and nature in one of these papers than in all Dickens' novels together," the financial results did not equal those accruing from one chapter by his great rival.

He spent much of his time in Paris, and was again, as he wrote to his mother, " bitten with my old painting mania." But he was learning wisdom, for he added, " and, as soon as I have written that famous book you know of and made a few hundred pounds, make a vow to the great gods that I will try the thing once more."

In London he saw a little of the Stirlings and Carlyle and received more than convivial sympathy from Harrison Ainsworth, then at the very height of his popularity and with his own magazine, in which Thackeray was asked to contribute a story by Major Gahagan.

But, in the following year, Fortune grew tired of tormenting him. Casually, and without premonition of the importance of the occasion, Jerrold introduced him to a little gentleman with a long nose and a hump-back. Courteously, Thackeray bowed and offered his hand to " Mr. Punch." The idea of a London rival to the Paris *Charivari* had originated some years earlier when Mayhew, Jerrold and Thackeray had discussed the idea, and even gone so far as to nominate the members of the staff. But a difference of opinion on finance, or possibly the absence of any, had resulted in the scheme being dropped, till 1841, when Jerrold and Mayhew put it into execution without Thackeray's assistance. Duly christened *Punch*, the hesitant enterprise was one of the few which was to survive the changing tastes of the century.

When Thackeray began, with his contributions called *Miss Tickletoby's Lectures on History*, the fate of *Punch* was sufficiently uncertain for the cautious Fitzgerald to warn him against contributing to it. But the real danger seems to have been to *Punch*, from " Miss Tickletoby." The public would laugh at most things, but a new journal could take no risks. The articles were discontinued, and it was not till 1843 that the long association between Thackeray and *Punch* began, to culminate in the success of both. Nevertheless, his *Paris Sketch Book* had not been written in vain, for in the year of " Miss Tickletoby's " death, Chapman & Hall commissioned him to visit Ireland with the object of writing a similar book on Irish topics.

Ireland being then engaged in one of her periodical revolts against England, it seemed a suitable time to commission a humorist to visit and report. Thackeray responded with alacrity, writing to Fitzgerald, on landing, a promising letter about " the filth and liberality " and fleas. But in addition to the latter, in which he seems to have been curiously interested throughout his life, he met Charles Lever, then fascinating the Dublin *beau monde* with his *Charles O'Malley* and *Harry Lorriquer*. Both convivially minded, good talkers, and sufficiently dissimilar in other respects, they became very cordial, and exchanged compliments, which were later forgotten when Thackeray wrote *Barry Lyndon* and Lever accused him of using his hospitality for the purpose of acquiring information with which to lampoon the Irish people. In the meantime there was no cloud between them, and when the book was published it was dedicated to Charles Lever – a doubtful compliment, when we read Thackeray's letter to his mother :

"The Book is going well. The Irish are in a rage about it."

With so many misunderstandings between the two peoples, a book seemed a small thing to be in a rage about, especially when it was selling well. But it did not make Thackeray either a fortune or a name, though he solicited and obtained a good "puff" from *Punch*.

Indeed, it looked almost as if he were condemned never to rise above the level of literary journalism. His fame, such as it then was, promised no higher destiny. Article-writing he had now in plenty, and even seems for a time to have held the position of sub-editor of the *Examiner*, for what it was worth – four guineas a week. But the publishers were busy with his rivals – Bulwer, Ainsworth, James and Dickens.

Nevertheless, he found much to enjoy in his life, and not least of his pleasures was a review, which he contributed to the *Pictorial Times*, of Disraeli's *Coningsby*. In agreement with the time-honoured practice, it began by attacking the author, proceeded to invite the public to laugh at him, paid a genuine, if rather hyperbolic compliment to one piece of characterisation, by a comparison of the author's satire with that of Juvenal, and proceeded to identify most of the characters with real people. The result was to set everyone reading *Coningsby* to discover everyone else's identity. The clubs resounded with chuckles and oaths and the success of the novel was assured.

It was undoubtedly from *Coningsby* that Thackeray borrowed the idea of using real people for the characters in his novels, and, as this feature of his work has been considered one of its worst blemishes, his supporters have rightly pointed out that the originator of the practice was Disraeli. But this is to say no more than that, though Thackeray omitted to set a bad example, he appreciated one enough to follow it.

In the Maginn school this sort of review was known as a " back-handed puff." But some people do not like " back-handers," and Disraeli seems to have been among their number. He had only a slight acquaintanceship with Thackeray, and, though the review helped to sell his novel, there is no evidence that it increased their cordiality.

Later, Disraeli retaliated for this and the parody of the book by Thackeray in *Punch's Prize Novelists*, by lampooning the lampooner under the title of St. Barbe in *Endymion*. Honour seems to have been satisfied, for they never spoke again.

In the intervals between these prize-fights, Thackeray rested and regaled himself, for when he joined the staff of *Punch* it was with a seat in the " Cabinet " that met weekly to decide on the cartoon.

Such meetings were much, but not exclusively, to Thackeray's liking. The eighteenth century had used its taverns, it is true, but it had also used its clubs, and the Mall, and the Pump Room at Bath. Still, the evenings were good of their kind. In the company of such good livers as Leach, Jerrold, à Beckett, Mayhew and others, there were cigars to smoke that were forbidden in the drawing-room, and jokes to tell that required the privacy of a man's world. It is remarked by a friend of Thackeray's who had sat with him at similar " Grub Street Nights' Entertainments," that " none of the little aside sermons which he preached in his books ever by any chance fell from his lips." One cannot be quite sure whether the remark is meant in disparagement or in praise, or merely in gratitude. And, in any case, Thackeray was still an acquisition, for, when called upon to do so, he was always ready to oblige the company with a song.

He had now rooms in Jermyn Street and had begun *Barry Lyndon*, the book of which he hoped that it might be his *Tom Jones* to Bulwer's *Clarissa*, and bring him the triumph over the scented popinjay that Fielding in the previous century had achieved over the pompous little whimpering Richardson.

During these days a rough diary indicates the premature fatigue which was so soon to affect both himself and his writing. He was undoubtedly drawing heavily upon his considerable but not inexhaustible strength. Again tradition steps in and murmurs that the absence of the restraining influence of his wife led him to excesses that hastened his death. It is kindly meant, this picture of the regrettable but pardonable excesses of the lonely man, seeking oblivion with head bowed over the walnuts and wine. But would oblivion come so easily to one who, before he met his wife, had learned with Maginn to hold his wine and scorn a " heel-tap " ? Or is it that the art of biography should consist in expressing great men in the terms of small ones ? Perhaps husbands may give the right inflection to that phrase " restraining influence." For the rest, though we may regret that he was not restrained from such ungenteel society, we may breathe relief that he was also not restrained from writing *Barry Lyndon*.

But, domestic isolation apart, his life just then was probably bleak enough. He had the entrée to two worlds and a home in neither. At the Procters' he could meet his literary peers, though all of them had bigger reputations ; in the tavern, his literary inferiors, though most of them were better paid. Slowly but inexorably he had been thrust from the position of an elegant young buck into that of a Grub Street drudge ; and when he visited the Cyder Cellars, now vanished from Maiden Lane, though he was received as the coming Rupert of Journalism, he must have often seen, through the drifting tobacco smoke, the ghost of " bright, broken Maginn," who had " drunk his cup a round or two before," and left both cup and colleagues, to creep silently to the Fleet Prison where drink and consumption had finished a career as promising as his pupil's when first it started.

Though Thackeray was always too sane to have gone to the same devil as Maginn, he must at that time have wondered whether he would ever rise above " the Doctor's " earthly throne, an editorial chair, or merely take his place therein to sit and scribble furiously against those who were passing him in the race for fame and wealth. For his was not a nature that wished to rule in hell, nor, for that matter, to serve in heaven. But between the two was a very comfortable compromise : the Mall, the club and the drawing-room – in short, the world that Major Pendennis so admired, enjoyed and adorned.

But he was " game," and in 1843 he induced *Fraser's* to try *Barry Lyndon* in serial form. With the new venture started, he embarked on his journey " from Cornhill to Cairo." The offer was made, to Chapman & Hall, to write a similar work to the *Paris* and *Irish Sketch Books*, the scene in this case being enlarged to include Jerusalem. The offer was accepted and, which was more immediately important, another made by the P. & O. Company, of a free passage.

The price of the book was to be £200, and it was written simultaneously with the " parts " of *Barry Lyndon* and his regular column for *Punch* from the Fat Contributor. But before he started he had Carlyle to contend with. Carlyle was angry. Thackeray was demeaning, not only himself, but the whole status of literature. " Further," the voice rumbled out of the Chelsea tub, "the trip resembled that of a blind fiddler going to and fro on a penny ferry-boat in Scotland, and playing tunes to the passengers for halfpence."

It has been affirmed that Thackeray accepted the rebuke with humility. Who, then, was the critic he replied to with some acerbity in an article in *Punch* entitled *Tait v. Titmarsh*? Charles Buller knew of Carlyle's words, for he repeated them to Thackeray with his endorsement of the sentiment. Perhaps it was he who quoted the phrase in *Tait's Magazine*. But a guess at their origin seems to lurk in the background of Thackeray's retorts about "Scotch fiddles," "bawbees" and "bagpipes," in *Tait v. Titmarsh* which also hints at some such similar suspicion in the concluding paragraph:

"I think he [the critic] must be a professional man of letters. It is only literary men nowadays who commit this suicidal form of impertinence; who sneak through the world ashamed of their calling, and show their independence by befouling the trade by which they live."

For a mood of humility, these are robust phrases, but the self-righteous sneer that provoked them needed stronger physic than humility. Indeed, Thackeray was never the man to offer the other cheek, nor, in those days of literary prize-fighting, would it have been quite safe to do so. Bulwer, in his prefaces, had tried a dignified, if rather mournful, self-defence against the critics, only to lead them on with whoops and cries to redouble their cudgelling. A man down was a man trodden on, and Thackeray had had too many kicks from Fortune to submit to those that could be repaid in kind.

This may explain his attitude a year earlier to an attack made on him in his own citadel, *Fraser's Magazine*. Such literary squabbles are as inevitable as they are unedifying, and this one deserves mention only for the light it throws on the *ad hominem* style of journalism of the day, and for the illuminating, if not too flattering portrait it gives of Thackeray's personal appearance. The article in question contained the following :

" The first person we met in the coffee-room was Bill Crackaway, one whom we have always looked upon as a bird of ill omen. His long, ungainly person is crowned with a face that Dame Nature must have fashioned just after making a bad debt and therefore in the worst of tempers. A countenance of preternatural longitude is imperfectly relieved by a nose on which the partial hand of Nature has lavished every beauty – length, breadth, thickness, all but a – bridge ; a mouth that seems suddenly arrested in the act of whistling, and from its conformation could only emanate a sinister sneer, but was physically incapable of the candour of an honest laugh, which, with a most inhuman squint, gave a rare finish to the *os frontis* of this Corinthian capital of our club."

Even had there been less loving care in the particularisation of all the features, the broken nose (received from Venables at Charterhouse) would have led to identification. Yet, taste apart, it is undoubtedly a not inaccurate picture of Thackeray as he looked and seemed to those who knew him only slightly. The more familiar picture, with white hair, fine forehead, and lips softened by success to a benevolence that neutralises the faintly sarcastic furrows from the nostrils to the mouth, was the latter-day image that England preserved of a man who had risen to rival Dickens, after years of competing with the Westmacotts, Hooks and Maginns.

His reply to the article was an ultimatum to *Fraser's*. Either the author of it, whom he identified as Deady Keane, ceased contributing to the magazine, or he would. For reason, he gave the abuse of what in his works he often calls " the sacred confidences of the mahogany." As this particular wood is no longer so popular as in those days, the idiom needs translating – the " mahogany " was the dining-table ; the law he invoked, the law of salt. Deady Keane was a colleague ; had wined, if he had not dined, with Thackeray ; had even shaken his hand but a week earlier.

Thackeray added that his decision was not intended as an act of retaliation against Keane, " but as an act of justice I owe myself and which is forced upon me." Whether the editor of *Fraser's* appreciated this nice point in etiquette, or merely thought that it was bad for the magazine to permit slanging-matches between members of its staff who were paid to slang novelists only, is not known. But the retaliation which Thackeray deprecated came, and Deady Keane went. There are those who may feel that the quality of the "justice he owed to himself" would have been more sublime had it been tempered by the mercy he declined to Keane, and others who will argue that his dignity would have been more evident had he insisted less upon it. It is difficult to decide such a point ; for, though with dignity a man frequently looks undignified, without it he will soon be made to feel so. Nevertheless, Thackeray had known what poverty was himself and how valuable a prop *Fraser's* could be. To remove it from a colleague seems a draconian remedy for an offence that might have been truly purged by an apology. But he was only thirty-two years old then, and, at thirty-two, egotists in general, and authors in particular, frequently exhibit an aggressiveness in direct proportion to their lack of success. He was later to taste the aggressiveness of others, when he himself was successful, and on the whole he swallowed it better than he did this first bewildering dose of his own medicine.

And he was still far from success when he sat on the deck of the P. & O. steamer on his way " from Cornhill to Cairo " and wrote three literary compositions simultaneously. The last " part " of *Barry Lyndon* was finished at Malta, but when he returned to England his Irish blackguard had been unable to make any sort of bow to the English public. Such a book could never compete with *Paul Clifford* or *Jack Sheppard*. That a rogue should also be a blackguard was mere cynicism. That, despite his blackguardism, he should compel a sneaking liking was immoral. The invincible virtue of the age was against both Barry and his creator. Villany, by all means – but genteel villany ; not this swaggering, wife-beating, card-sharping blackguard, who finished, not on his knees, but in the Fleet. And gentle birth there must be, not a lying tongue to claim it and dupe both men and women with a pedigree so faked as to be perilously like many recently purchased from the Heralds, to figure armorially on the carriage doors which Mr. Yellowplush opened outside the church.

So one of Thackeray's most polished works passed unnoticed. It was the voice of Fielding echoing against an historical background greater than any Scott had painted, and dying away unheard in an England agog to catch the stage whispers of Bulwer and Ainsworth.

Fortunately for Thackeray, he was also a humorous writer for *Punch*. The Fat Contributor had best keep to his homely jokes about sea-sickness, fleas, bathing-machines and bugs, and leave the eighteenth century, with its gaming, duelling and elegance, to those who had a taste for such things. And in the eighteen-forties they were remarkably few.

CHAPTER IV

The Brookfields and their circle – Thackeray and Mrs. Brookfield – *Jeames's Diary* – *The Book of Snobs* – Carlyle's opinion of Thackeray – the first number of *Vanity Fair*.

THACKERAY was a great letter-writer, but, except in the case of Fitzgerald, he seldom wrote to men. It was his women friends who received the long, whimsical, sometimes trenchant, often egotistical but always interesting letters. Tradition ascribes this to the good habits inculcated by his mother, and sentiment to the great need of an outlet for the confidences he would have given to a wife. Without contradicting either tradition or sentiment, one may add a quality within himself – a certain queer timidity, not infrequently to be found associated with a little too robust a cheerfulness and with a clarity of mind that sees too easily through the stout pretences which comfort less fastidious natures. For all his love of the eighteenth century, one feels that had he been born therein there would have come to him moments when he would have stolen away, a little timidly, from a Pope or a Walpole, to clutch the hands of a Johnson or a Goldsmith. And with women we see the same duality of attraction. In Becky Sharp and Beatrix Esmond he shows a truly subtle understanding of a type of woman more common in the eighteenth than in the nineteenth century. But when he meets them he is not quite at ease. True, he adopts the attitude of a gallant. Temporarily borrowing a rapier, he bows to them with a faint but meaning smile, only to shake his head and laugh a little nervously, and throw away his sword to offer an arm and an umbrella to the Lauras and Helens of *Pendennis* or the Amelias of *Vanity Fair*.

And in the wife of his old Cambridge friend, W. H. Brookfield, he met a woman whom he certainly used as the model for Amelia in *Vanity Fair* and probably as Elizabeth in *Lovel the Widower*. Between these two books he fell in love with her, and between these two characters lies hers, who was his " dear lady."

The association began when he had moved into St. James's Street and the Rev. W. H. Brookfield had not yet put to their full use those gifts of oratory to which his friend Kinglake pays so high a tribute, in the words :

" An orator of original genius, he possessed marvellous histrionic skill which he was able to moderate in the pulpit."

His wife, Jane, was the niece of the historian, Hallam, from which fortuitous circumstance, rather than by any great intellectual qualities, one feels that she and her husband found their way into the society of such figures as the Tennysons, the Hallams, Kinglake, Carlyle, Landor, Monckton Milnes, Lord Lyttelton, and Thackeray. Brookfield himself (the Rev. Honeyman of *The Newcomes*) is an ambiguous figure. He wrote innumerable letters to everyone, full of little stories (quite decorous) of " swell " dinners to which he had been invited, of the " select " nature of his congregation, of the " utter trash " that Dickens wrote, of the effect of his sermons upon his flock, and of his fears that a visiting divine might recognise a sermon that he had " cribbed " from him.

Yet his friends called him a scholar and a wit, and Kinglake could say : " Ever generous, indulgent, large-minded, Brookfield was never demoralised by Holy Orders." The effect upon Holy Orders is not stated.

But the collaborators in *Mrs. Brookfield and her Circle* do much to explain the ambiguous clergyman when they say :

" We hope we have not wronged the writers by suppressing too rigorously the letters which give the more serious side of their natures – a side they all possessed. Their bright *bavardage*, it is true, occasionally obscures the affection that lurks beneath their words, but such genial chatter must not always be taken *au serieux*."

Perhaps this applies also to the testimonials which the " circle " seem to have been in the habit of giving to one another periodically, and which read so often like the ceremonial titles of an Eastern potentate.

But Brookfield never got outside his circle. The Bishopric of Barbados was the only firm offer made to him as an official testimony to his gifts. And Barbados was such a long way away, for a man who had clung assiduously to the " right " people from Cambridge down to the crypt of his church, where Thackeray shows him living as the Rev. Honeyman and describes as "a fellow with a very smooth tongue and sleek, sanctified exterior. He was rather a popular preacher and used to cry a good deal in the pulpit."

The picture we get from his letters is that of a good-natured, convivial, facetious little man, whose religion was distinguished by a simple, unaffected insincerity. With his lovely but rather enigmatic wife, we see him acting in private the communal Boswell to a circle of nineteenth-century Johnsons, and in his pulpit exhibiting the pliancy without the adroitness of a Pepys. Yet he was warmly liked by such different characters as Tennyson, Carlyle and Kinglake, which seems to show that out of his pulpit he had qualities which unsuited him to enter it. There have been many such clergymen both before and since.

His wife, judged by her portrait by George Richmond, fulfilled the claims made for her looks. For her disposition we must look elsewhere, and first to her letters to Thackeray. Most of them betray the rôle of the simple miss, in faintly coquettish awe of the famous writer. But here and there peeps out a little spirit, as when she tells him :

"What an odd girl Adelaide Procter is ! I should give her a little quiet set-down some day if I were you. I think it would be friendly and do her good. Do you think me very spiteful to-day ?"

Et

She could also write of *Vanity Fair*, though not to him, that she wished he would " give Amelia a little more brains."

The friendship began with a dinner at the Brookfields, developed into the habit of Thackeray's taking Saturday breakfasts with them, and produced a big bundle of letters, most of which have been published, but all of which, we are assured, " redound to the credit of all parties concerned." From what we see of the beautiful but rather enigmatic Mrs. Brookfield, we find no difficulty in believing it. Indeed, tradition seems to have been a little presumptive with Mrs. Brookfield. She has been promoted to the position of that essential figure in the lives of all great men – the woman who either makes or mars them. Actually, Mrs. Brookfield performed neither service for Thackeray. What she seems to have done, very circumspectly, was to make him look rather foolish. When, in the evening of his life, he sat down to pay off old scores in *Lovel the Widower*, we recognise the thinly disguised *dramatis personnæ* and catch an echo of the outgrown folly :

" I daresay you are beginning to suppose that out of all this crying and sentimentality which a soft-hearted old fool of a man poured out to a young girl – out of all this whimpering and pity, something which is akin to pity might arise. But in this, my good madam, you are utterly wrong. Some people have the smallpox twice ; *I do not.* . . . If I chose to put my grief in a ridiculous light, why not ? Why do you suppose that I am going to make a tragedy of such an old, used up, battered, stale, vulgar, trivial, everyday subject as a jilt who plays with a man's passions and laughs at him and leaves him?"

But he was fifty-one when that was written, and a prey to a disease that attacked him with spasms of pain in increasing frequency. At thirty-five, life looks different, and who could have resisted so charming a creature as was Jane Brookfield at the age of twenty-four? She had been brought up with a back straightened by two hours daily on the "back-board," and the additional support of a " spider " – a form of genteelly sadistic corset of iron, covered with leather, which effectively prevented too languishing a poise – while, to keep the gentle head from drooping, a piece of holly had been pinned to her little pinafore, just beneath the chin. She gives her own artless story of her first meeting with the man, eleven years her senior in age and already so many more years older in experience. Her husband brought him home to dinner unexpectedly.

"There was fortunately," she says, "a good plain dinner, but I was young and shy enough to feel embarrassed because we had no sweets, and I privately sent my maid to the nearest confectioner to bring a dish of tartlets, which I thought would give a finish to our simple meal. When they were placed before me I timidly offered our guest a small one, saying, 'Will you have a tartlet, Mr. Thackeray?' 'I will, but I'll have a twopenny one, if you please,' he answered, so beamingly that we all laughed and my shyness disappeared."

It is a pretty picture, and shows Thackeray at his best, but is there not in the narrative of the lady herself a shade too much ingenuousness? Her references to her " youth and shyness " and the " simple meal " and her " timidity " – are they solely the convention of the age, or older arts that yet remain so perennially new? But why spoil the picture by such enquiries? It was spoilt ultimately by the not unwarrantable jealousy of her husband. In the interim it yielded a great deal of joy to Thackeray himself, and to posterity a collection of his published letters, half-tender, half-jocular, and more revealing than any he wrote to any other person, man or woman.

For five years the association lasted, and Thackeray at one time even offered his rather poor friends, who were reduced to inhabiting the crypt of the Rev. W. H. Brookfield's church, quarters in his own house till they could " find other lodgment." But Mrs. Brookfield gently, and on the whole discreetly, declined the offer. For, despite his *bavardage*, the Rev. Brookfield was not always too happy at the attentions paid by Thackeray to his wife. These attentions, indeed, led to an exchange of views between the two men, when Thackeray declared :

" Her innocence, looks, angelical sweetness and kindness charm and ravish me to the highest degree ; and every now and then in contemplating them I burst out into uncouth raptures. They are not in the least dangerous – it is a sort of artistic delight (a spiritual sensuality, so to speak)."

There is urgent need of a glossary of early-Victorian eloquence to help those who have to extract from so lofty an idiom its exact meaning. Fortunately, in this case Thackeray himself translates, by adding more simply:

"Well, I've opened my bowels to you. Indeed, there has not been much secret before and I've always admired the generous spirit in which you have witnessed my queer raptures. If I had envy or what you call passion, or a wicked thought . . . I should have cut you years ago."

This "opening of the bowels" reassured the clergyman, who could also comfort himself with the knowledge that there was no need to worry about his wife till his friend cut him; and, as by that time it would be too late, there was no real need to worry at all.

Meanwhile, *From Cornhill to Cairo* was published, well received and sold well – a sequence of events sufficiently novel to Thackeray to make him more amused than angry at the single dissentient critic, who called him "a heartless, self-sufficient Cockney."

About this time, too, *Vanity Fair* was begun – not as a novel, but as "Pen and Pencil Sketches of English Society."

Thackeray had been commissioned by Colborne, the too enterprising publisher of Bulwer's successes, to write a story for publication in "parts" in Colborne's own paper, the *New Monthly*. With an advance already paid and a " part " already written, Colborne enterprisingly sold the magazine to Harrison Ainsworth, retaining the MS. he was not prepared to publish in book form and could no longer, serially, in a magazine he had sold. He even seems to have been enterprising enough to ask for the " advance " back before returning the MS. Thackeray wrote three letters of increasing exacerbation to Ainsworth, for news of his MS. and a decision as to its fate. Ultimately, Ainsworth replied apologetically, making amends by offering to publish in his newly acquired magazine the incomplete and derelict story. Thackeray was placed in a most difficult position, for, getting no reply to his letters, he had composed and sent to press for *Punch* an article in the *Fraserian* vein, lampooning both Ainsworth and his magazine – the one for accepting and the other for containing piffling articles by titled scribblers, to the exclusion of good articles by writers less well known socially. He hurriedly wrote, making " a clean breast of it," to Ainsworth, adding : " I shouldn't have lifted my hand to smite my friend had explanations come earlier, so that now *you* must be called upon to play the part of forgiver, in which I am sure you'll shine." And Ainsworth, to his credit, " shone " and " forgave." Indeed, the capacity for forgiveness must have been a necessary quality in any man who wished to remain friends with Thackeray ; for to the sharp-edged egotism of the man was added a quality in riposte that was frequently cruel and at times caddish. Yet, paradoxically, it is his vices that proclaim his virtues. For one man to forgive caddishness in another, he must find some other qualities correspondingly large. In the protean nature of Thackeray we see hints of many such qualities, of kindness, affection, humour and courage. But it is perhaps in his description by Carlyle that we detect that composite character which led other men not to take too seriously the man who took himself quite seriously enough :

"There is," said Carlyle, " a great deal of talent in him, a great deal of sensibility – irritability, sensuality, vanity without limit – and nothing or little but sentimentalism and play-actorism to guide it all with ; not a good or well-found ship in such waters on such a voyage."

Allowing a little for Carlyle's notoriously bad digestion, it is a picture that fits the man. If we attempt to assess him in terms of the personalities he so admired in his lectures on the English humorists of the eighteenth century, we might say that he had, in part, the urbanity of Addison, the robustness of Fielding, the humour of Hogarth, the nervous irritability of Johnson, the sentiment of Steele, the slyness of Sterne, the cruelty of Pope, and a little, but only a little, of the heart of Goldsmith. Never completely the equal of any one of these, as he might have been if he would have been more completely himself, he contained enough of the best of each to be at most times likeable and at some times lovable, and – through his own incompleteness – at all times a little pitiable.

With Ainsworth forgiving, Thackeray sent him

a story, retaining the half-written, half-paid-for and as yet unpublished MS. of *Vanity Fair*. But before this " unwanted child " had been licked into shape its author had written for *Punch Jeames's Diary*, a skit on the railway mania in the idiom of Mr. Yellowplush, and his first " Christmas book," *Mrs. Perkin's Ball*. Both were successes and were followed by a greater.

In February 1846 there appeared in *Punch*, the first of the *Snob Papers*. They continued to appear, with ever-increasing popularity, for twelve months, and in the last month of the twelve was published the first number of *Vanity Fair*. The book that was to make his name, and establish him to the title of genius, appeared in fortnightly " parts," in yellow covers to distinguish it from the green of Dickens.

Henceforth the rival colours were to become the badges of rival factions, each claiming for their master the pre-eminence which neither claimed (publicly) for himself. But *Vanity Fair* was slow in moving, and it was *The Book of Snobs* that brought Thackeray the fame his starved egotism craved. With one appetite satisfied, another intruded, for he writes jubilantly :

" I think if I can make a push at the present moment – if my friends will shout ' Titmarsh for ever ' . . . I may go up with a run to a pretty fair place in my trade and be allowed to appear before the public as among the first violins.

" But," he adds, " my tunes must be heard in the streets and organs must grind them."

As we catch a glimpse of him now, flushed with

the success he had waited fourteen years to taste, we may recall, with faint misgivings, the dyspeptic verdict of Carlyle :

" Not a good or well-found ship in such waters, on such a voyage."

CHAPTER V

Accusations of snobbery – his children join him in London – the slow progress of Vanity Fair *– Charlotte Brontë's dedication of* Jane Eyre *to Thackeray – scandal and success.*

EVEN the Athenians grew tired of hearing Aristides called "the Just." Similarly it was inevitable that the author of *The Book of Snobs* should ultimately be accused of being one. Analogy seemed on the side of the accusers. As a Eurasian has the strongest colour-prejudice, so a man who most reviled snobs must have snob blood in his veins. And his actions seemed to support the accusation. For what happened to the novelist who had been castigating society, once he succeeded in making society listen to his philippics? Did he not straightway join them and their flunkeys in their " routs " and their vanities? And he had not been too gentle in his castigations. Though written with a faintly contemptuous good humour, the *Snob* sermons were pretty hard-hitting. He had used a rapier, but he had used it as a cutlass. Such a man was more likely to make enemies than friends ; and such a man, no matter how delicately he trod, was bound sooner or later to share the fate of Agag. And he did not even trouble to tread delicately. When society, a little puzzled, but on the whole more amused than angry, smiled at him, he bowed elegantly. As the doors of the *beau monde* opened to receive him, he advanced, not with vulgar haste, but with a more exasperating nonchalance. As they closed behind his tall figure, a howl went up from those who were left outside – " Snob ! " In response, he merely smiled and shrugged his shoulders.

For snobbery consisted not in being in the *beau monde*, but in being uncomfortable in it. And as he was, personally, not uncomfortable in it, all good snobs should have admitted that he could be no snob, who had never known the real pleasures of snobbery. For discomfort was undoubtedly one of them. When a congenital snob entered an hereditary mansion, it was only by the discomfort of feeling " out of it " that he could appreciate that he was really in it. Though the poet of the day was acclaimed when he wrote " Kind hearts are more than coronets," those who acclaimed him were, nevertheless, assured that the two went very well together.

With this view, Thackeray disagreed, not as a general proposition, but in the particular instance of the snob. So he wrote *The Book of Snobs* to show, not only that human worth was measured by the size of a footman's calves, and female chastity by the weight of a *roué's* coronet, but that, despite this system of ready-reckoning, married daughters were frequently unhappy and plush footmen always expensive. It was a practical rather than a moral view, for Thackeray was always distinguished more by a quality of radiant commonsense than by the sublime glow of moral indignation.

Indignation he knew, but it was roused by the fool, not by the knave. It was never the humbug that he lampooned. He could make a hero or a heroine of a humbug, as with Barry Lyndon and Becky Sharp. We have no generic term for the type that roused Thackeray, sometimes to scorn, more often to a Voltairean laughter. For he attacked, not the humbug who, for some good reason, pretended to be what he was not, but the fool who, with no good reason, really thought he was what he pretended to be. A woman like Becky Sharp who, in a wealthy world, had no wealth but her wits and could yet take and hold her position in society, not only amused him, but aroused his admiration. But the banker-Newcomes who, despite their banking-assets, really believed that when they left their bank for Lord Cinqbar's drawing-room they were no longer bankers, he derides with all the power of his invective.

It was all such fools that he called "snobs," and he attacked them, not because they deceived the world by their pretensions, but merely because they deceived themselves.

When *Vanity Fair* set all educated England talking, it set some saying that in the book "all the good people were fools and all the clever ones knaves." Actually, of course, they were not. In *Vanity Fair* all the fools are good and all the knaves clever, which is a different thing. For Thackeray saw morality mainly as a matter of income. It was not Becky but her creator who exclaimed: "It is so easy to be good on £2,000 a year." It was his whole reading of life, as his whole philosophy was acceptance of life, and his sole tribute to it a faint pity. But the pity was for the knave, not for the fool. It was a sort of sinners' creed, and produced the magnificent sermons of *Barry Lyndon* in defence of dicing and cards, in a world that lived by the same methods, but called them " share-dealing " and " commercial enterprise." The hypocrisy of such humbugs as Becky never roused Thackeray as did the hypocrisy of the world which compelled her to be a hypocrite if she would continue to live in it.

He wrote once to Mrs. Brookfield :

" If I mayn't tell you what I feel, what is the use of a friend ? That's why I would rather have a sad letter from you, or a short one if you are tired and unwell, than a sham one – and I don't subscribe at all to the doctrine of ' striving to be cheerful.' *A quoi bon,* convulsive grins and humbugging good humour ? Let us have a reasonable cheerfulness and melancholy too, if there is occasion for it – and no more hypocrisy in life than need be."

Unfortunately, quite a lot was needed in his day, and because, as an eminently sane man, he used as much of it " as need be," he was pilloried by those who used little else.

He would have liked to see a world good enough for the Amelias to live in ; but common sense told him that this world was not, and worldly wisdom that it never would be. His Barry and his Becky, like their creator, took the world as they found it, and their faults were the measure of its cruelties more truly than were Amelia's little arts a proof of its kindness.

So he fitted Becky for the world she was put into. It was left to Dickens to put into the world women who were more truly fitted for the world to come.

Such was Thackeray's philosophy, and as such it was too cynical for an age that had brought the optimism and morals of the newly genteel into the last citadel of a dying aristocracy. Had the word been coined, he would have called himself a " realist " ; as it was not, he let his age call him a satirist. More truly was he a caricaturist – a Bernard Shaw without any faith in progress. But he also lacked Shaw's impersonal basis for his views. In Thackeray, most of his invective was due to personal resentment. Though in that queer fragment, *On Going to See a Man Hanged*, he could speak with an almost Shavian sanity and conviction, most of his anathemas reflected the slights society had put upon him, as much as the indignities it did to human nature as a whole.

In *The Book of Snobs*, he was castigating purse-pride, but he was doing so largely as the result of the purse-shame he had felt himself, with all the intensity of a fastidious nature, during years of toil and poverty.

For he had both by nature and culture a real love of the eighteenth century, and what was left of that age was to be found in the drawing-rooms of the few, besieged by the many who, replete with mushroom crests upon their carriage doors and Mr. Yellowplush mounted in powdered rectitude behind them, drove the streets on their way to the *beau monde*, splashing with their genteel mud the outcast journalist on his way to the Cyder Cellars. And the Cyder Cellars was not his spiritual home. Even if he had not been born into the fashionable world, he had been born into a very comfortable one till the Hon. Deuceace drove him out of it in his cabriolet on the way to his bankers, leaving him to complete the journey to Grub Street on foot.

When, with no help but his own pen and courage, he came into his own again, it was inevitable that his satire should wilt, but he could, with some plausibility, meet the charge of snobbery with the retort that in entering the *beau monde* he entered, not as a parvenu, but as a prodigal.

His real apostasy was not then, nor in turning snob, but later and in turning " soft." The genius which had struck out such brilliant sparks against the flints of adversity, softened with success. Though it cannot be said that he entered Vanity Fair to scoff and stayed to pray, it must be admitted that among its booths he found too much to amuse and please him for him ever to wish to walk out again. He was soon to write that letter to his mother, affirming that there were " a hundred good reasons for a lazy, liberal, costly – but not extravagant – way of life." Of that hundred, he hints at one in his lecture on Addison :

" He likes to sit in the smoking-room at the

'Grecian' or the 'Devil,' to pace 'Change and the Mall, to mingle in that great club of the world, sitting alone in it somehow."

Before his death he grew to know intimately that " great club of the world," but his tragedy as a man was that he was never quite happy " sitting alone in it," and his tragedy as an artist that he spent his genius in paying for his seat.

That such a work as *The Book of Snobs* was successful may seem a greater surprise than that its author could be accused of diagnosing his own disease. Yet its success was inevitable. It had the melancholy fate of all works that seek to castigate vice. To do so it had to reveal vice, and in revealing vice it attracted the vicious. No moralist has ever yet overcome this practical difficulty. Though written as a jeremiad against the snobs, it became their vade-mecum. It showed them what to do in bidding them not to do it. If it touched a few snobbish hearts to repent of their gentility, it stimulated many more to be firm in their faith. For, if one were accused of having thrust oneself into Lord Cinqbar's drawing-room, such an accusation was also an admission that one had been seen there.

The infamous paper, the *Age*, had already discovered by its circulation that its readers would rather see their names in a scandal than not see them in print. If the parvenu papa could regard his son's entry into the *beau monde* as so important that it did not matter if the boy took the easiest path through the fashionable gambling " hells," the Turf or the society of " bruisers " and their fashionable sponsors, and was ready to pay the cost of these modish " wild oats " in the sure knowledge that he paid on behalf of his son the same sort of bills that Lord Cinqbar paid for his, then a *Book of Snobs* must have sent him seeking for his own likeness as pleasurably as he sought in Debrett's the title of his son's spendthrift associates and his daughter's profligate wooers. Even the virtuous enjoyed it, since, having no fear that they might find their own portraits therein, they could devote their entire energies to identifying their neighbours'.

So *The Book of Snobs*, written as satire, became a social success. It was unfortunate, but we cannot blame Thackeray.

He was now affluent enough to gratify the quite unsnobbish desire to have his children with him, and meeting with slight opposition from his mother, who wished to keep them with her in Paris, even went so far as to offer her and his step-father and grandmother a harbourage in his new house at 13 Young Street, Kensington Square.

With a boyish eagerness, he writes to his mother :

" There are two capital bedrooms, and a little sitting-room for you and G.P. [short for Grandpapa, the title he always gave his step-father] – a famous bedroom for G.M. [his grandmother] on the first floor. . . . There's a good downstairs and a dining-room and drawing-room and a little courtyard and garden and a little greenhouse, and

FT

Kensington Gardens at the gate, and omnibuses every two minutes. What more can a mortal want ? "

This is unpardonable enthusiasm for a cynic and can only be explained by the supposition that inside the great bulk of the man lay a little core of very English sentiment ; and, behind the " sinister sneer " that Deady Keane had seen, a quality of faint timidity that had called for some concealment during his fourteen years' lonely sojourn among the booths of Vanity Fair.

But only the children came to him, which was, on the whole, more convenient. His mother was beginning to show interest in a very concentrated form of Christianity, and his step-father was reaching the age when he had little to do but re-fight in memory old battles, both on the field and in journalism and banking. Still, Thackeray had a " house-warming," attended by the old soldier, to which he also invited the Brookfields, Kinglake, and one at least of his Cyder Cellars friends – Leech of *Punch*.

Meanwhile, *Vanity Fair* was appearing in " parts " and attracting very little attention. Its appeal was to a class of readers who preferred their novels whole, and its fame at the mercy of reviewers who rarely condescended to do more than " notice " novels published in " parts " – except those by Dickens. But there was still *Mrs. Perkin's Ball* to show by its sales, which were bigger than any he had ever known, that a satirist must also be human and, when possible, facetious – a lesson which, unfortunately, he took to heart.

And then in quick succession two women rushed to his assistance. The first was the staunch Mrs. Procter, who cajoled, bullied and finally induced the *Edinburgh* to review *Vanity Fair*. The *Edinburgh*, being Scottish, was suspicious. The editor, Abraham Hayward, was worse – he was rather stupid. Fortunately, he was also quite timid. The situation was critical. The *Edinburgh* never noticed a novel published in " parts." If it could be induced to notice this one – in the right spirit – Thackeray's fortune was made. Mrs. Procter rose to the occasion, and above it. She practically dictated to Hayward the review he was to write.

He wrote it, and, when he found he had " backed a winner," gained so sudden an access of confidence and courage that he claimed to have " discovered " the book, and wrote to Thackeray that he (Thackeray) had " already beaten Dickens out of the inner circles."

And this was true. The *beau monde*, particularly the ladies within it, welcomed Thackeray, not with open arms, which was taboo, but with open doors and smiling requests for his autograph.

Thackeray responded with alacrity, despite Carlyle, who was again gloomy and despondent at the picture of a literary man so demeaning himself – not, on this occasion, with a fiddle on a ferry-boat, but by becoming a candle-flame for *beau-mondaine* moths to flutter round.

Fitzgerald himself, a little uneasy at the picture

of his Titmarsh following Mr. Yellowplush into
Lord Cinqbar's drawing-room, repeated the Highland dirge to Thackeray, who answered unspleenfully :

"I can't eat more dinners than I did last year
and dine at home with my dear little women
three times a week ; but two or three great people
ask me to their houses, and 'Vanity Fair' does
everything except pay."

This unsatisfactory feature was remedied by
another woman, for in 1848 appeared a new
edition of a very salacious novel called *Jane Eyre*,
written by one Currer Bell, whose sex even was
unknown, or only guessed at with horror by the
North British Review in the words : " If *Jane Eyre*
be the production of a woman, she must be a
woman unsexed." For this book had revealed a
quality in human nature that had been completely
outgrown since the eighteenth century. In *Jane
Eyre* a man and a woman were quite unmistakably depicted as having more than a spiritual
attraction for each other. And, as if this were
not degrading enough, the emotion thus suggested
was as strong in the woman as in the man.
Though recognised as a work of genius, this " tale
of passion," as it was described by the publishers,
shocked many of the critics who were unaccustomed to heroines with carnal emotions.

And the second edition confirmed their worst
suspicions. It was dedicated to Thackeray. The
coincidence was too great to be accidental. Was
he not, like Rochester, married to a wife who had
lost her reason ? And had he not young children

who needed a governess and would most certainly have had one supplied when her presence was required for another purpose?

The *Quarterly Review* hit exactly the right note in saying that the author of *Jane Eyre* was probably a woman " who, for some sufficient reason, has long forfeited the society of her own sex." The dedication to Thackeray was the " sufficient reason." The bewildered satirist was credited with possessing a mistress who had also written the most improper book of the century.

With a truly horrifying archness, Currer Bell kept up the mystery by maintaining an anonymity which, while shielding her, only the more cruelly exposed Thackeray, who was in complete ignorance of the identity of his admirer. For *Jane Eyre*, despite male horror, had found its way into the feminine world, silencing the piano and the duet, ousting the sampler and the crochet-hook, tinging innocent cheeks with a most becoming blush, banishing the serenity from tender eyes and filling loving little hearts with emotions, indecorous, unelevating, but wholly delightful.

When Thackeray, ready to be fashionably satirical, entered a drawing-room, the little heads inclined together and the little tongues whispered, and the great cynical " lion " shuddered to find himself, not only famous, but deliciously infamous. Still, his infamy swelled his fame, for it helped to sell *Vanity Fair*.

And, all the while, the innocent and safely anonymous Currer Bell had no erotic yearnings towards the author whom she described as " the first social regenerator of his day." She effected his own " social regeneration " a while later, by revealing her identity, whereupon Thackeray sent to Miss Charlotte Brontë a presentation copy of *Vanity Fair*, with his " grateful regards."

CHAPTER VI

Relations between Thackeray and Dickens – the effect of Dickens' work on Thackeray's – increasing popularity – quarrel with Charles Lever – Pendennis – illness – accusations of lampooning old Fraserian colleagues.

THACKERAY was now famous – the equal in repute, though not in popularity, of Dickens. The partisanship which soon developed between the supporters of the two greatest novelists of the day was not reflected in their attitude towards each other. Though never friends, they were always cordial until the quarrel over Yates and the Garrick Club parted them for all but the last year of Thackeray's life. Their children frequently entertained each other, and several such parties at Dickens' house, followed by amateur theatricals, were attended by Thackeray and enjoyed with that rambustious abandon which he frequently showed when good spirits and good health were with him.

But by the nature of the two men and the quality of their work they could meet seldom and mingle never. Thackeray had moved into the world of fashion, while Dickens remained always essentially middle class, both in tastes and habits. They had as a common meeting-place that sort of literary no-man's-land, between journalism and letters, wherein critics and authors mingle and forget, over their wine, which of them is the more important in a realm that needs the best of both.

Thackeray has been accused of jealousy of Dickens, but there is no evidence of it. Though his public utterances naturally contain that studied enthusiasm which both politeness and policy would suggest to a man sufficiently confident of his own qualities to fear an accusation of jealousy if he decried his rival, there was, in his tribute in one of his lectures, enough criticism to guarantee its sincerity.

" I may quarrel," he says, " with Mr. Dickens' art a thousand and a thousand times. I delight and wonder at his genius."

This tribute Dickens gratefully acknowledged and posterity has reluctantly confirmed. And Thackeray continued to " delight and wonder " at his rival's genius. Unfortunately, he was also influenced by it. Reading the death of Paul Dombey, he exclaimed : " There is no writing against this ; one hasn't an atom of chance. It is stupendous."

Though we may agree with the first sentiment, it is doubtful if Thackeray really believed the second. For Dickens was in complete sympathy with his age, while Thackeray was always in dumb and, at his best, in vocal revolt from it. And the age liked its women pure, its men noble, its villains bad, its humour spiced with red noses and gin, and its tears plentiful but not too salt – in other words, it liked all its emotions undiluted and all its characters unmixed. And Thackeray made the fatal mistake of blending both good and bad qualities in the same character, which rightly called down on him the reproach of being in this respect like Shakespeare and Fielding, who, in common with himself, " exhibit the marks of the beast in the best, and the traits of goodness in the worst, specimens of human nature."

It was so confusing. With Uriah Heep you knew exactly where you stood. He was always the same – humble and evil. With Colonel Altamont, you were all at sea. The blackguard would sponge and threaten you with blackmail, and then, a while later, when times were better with him and worse with you, offer you, a little sheepishly, a five-pound note to see you through. Whatever slights seedy journalism put upon Thackeray, they gave him a marvellous insight into the furtive creed of the underdog. But the public that read Dickens disliked blurred outlines. The underdog was "under," and if he wished to come to the top he must not, like Colonel Altamont, show fragmentary traces of virtue, but, like Micawber, change his whole nature, or, like Nancy, arrange to be murdered with a recently memorised prayer on her lips. In short, Thackeray got inside the skins of his characters ; Dickens never did more than get into the clothes of his.

But Dickens knew how to cry and Thackeray did not. And weeping is not easy in fiction, unless performed for its own sake. Sir Leslie Stephen has defined the sentimentalist as one " who does not weep because painful thoughts are thrust upon him, but because he finds weeping pleasant in itself." And Dickens, as much as his public, enjoyed a " good cry," and the tears they both shed were the pleasant and refreshing tears of English sentiment ; tears of good digestion, honest lives and whole hearts ; tears that left no stains, either on the cheeks or the character. It was genuine, spontaneous sentimentalism, introduced as part of the technique of the novel – as " comic relief " was introduced into melodrama, and with the same intent : to prevent either novel or melodrama from becoming too close to life.

And Thackeray could not cry. Unfortunately, he felt he ought to. It was not merely a question of competing with Dickens. He saw that, in great art, tears had their place and meaning, and was misguided enough to believe that for that reason no work of art was great without them. What he did not realise was that in his genius was no quality either of the tragic or the pathetic. *King Lear* bored him and *Hamlet* was only a stage full of dead people when the curtain dropped. Mixed with much artistic sensibility was a leaven of English philistinism akin to Fielding's, whom Taine called the " good buffalo." But Thackeray lacked Fielding's " compactness " of character. It was not for nothing that he had all his life " parodied " other writers. For parody, though founded upon ridicule, may be modified by admiration till it becomes emulation. Thackeray did not weep to order, nor for profit, but he probably wept because he was being constantly compared with Dickens and reproved for his cynicism. But, whatever the reason, his tears were disastrous. They were not sentimental; they were meretricious.

Yet, curiously, they were real enough to him. When Helen Pendennis died he really cried over her, and when Colonel Newcome died he wrote a letter to a friend, full of self-conscious sentiment and wry attempts to smile through his tears. The explanation of this lies in the fact that the pathos of Helen Pendennis and Colonel Newcome did not grow out of their lives in the novels, but out of Thackeray's emotions towards their prototypes in real life. When Helen and the Colonel died he wept for the imagined deaths of his mother and step-father. It was part of the price he paid for drawing people from his own life instead of from the life he saw about him. For what he said of Addison might, with but slight alteration, have been said with equal truth of himself:

"He does not go very deep: let gentlemen of a profound genius, accustomed to the plunge of the bathos, console themselves by thinking he *couldn't* go very deep. There are no traces of suffering in his writing. He was so good, so honest, so cheerfully selfish, if I may use the word."

Thackeray in good health was "so good, so honest, so healthy, so cheerfully selfish." In bad health there were "traces of suffering in his writing," but it was a rather querulous "suffering," personal and vindictive at times – never tragical or pathetic, and never quite convincing. When his characters are sad they are inclined to whimper, and when they whimper it is their author's sorrows they prate of, not their own. If

Thackeray, with his essentially unreligious nature, had any Bible at all, it was Ecclesiastes – never the Book of Job. Divine despair was too bitter a brew for a man with a taste for claret.

A less earnest age would have accepted his limitations, admired his splendid gifts and asked no more of him than that he should stand with Molière ; one more critical might have urged him to develop his genius and take his place with Voltaire ; none should have expected him to rank with Swift ; and only his own could have whimpered at him to rival Dickens.

He wrote once that " among Dickens' superiorities over me is the fecundity of his imagination." In attempts to enrich his work in this respect, Thackeray neglected his own art, which was interpretative and panoramic, and consisted in bringing to life a " class " against a background that was historic, cosmopolitan and patrician, for the totally different art of Dickens, which was creative and pictorial, and brought to life the " type " against a background that was parochial, insular and middle class.

Indeed, Dickens was bringing to perfection that essentially nineteenth-century product, the novel with a story and the story with a purpose. Thackeray's whole genius lay with the picaresque writers, such as Fielding, who took a number of people and a number of incidents and wove the whole into a brilliant pattern, with no more purpose than the exhibition of the humanities, and no more moral than can be extracted from a not too moral world.

Nevertheless, we cannot blame Dickens for the thwarting of his rival's genius, nor, indeed, entirely the public, of whom Thackeray said in one lecture:

" Mere satiric art is addressed to a class of readers and thinkers quite different from the simple souls who laugh and weep over the novel."

The real cause was in part Thackeray's health, which so soon after success began to give way ; in part the natural indolence (made more pronounced by illness) which left him always writing against time and often against inclination ; and lastly, the lack of what can only be called " literary integrity."

Even Trollope could admit that, despite his brilliant gifts, Thackeray never quite did justice to himself, though Trollope ascribes the cause principally to his illness.

But, both in his letters and in his famous preface to *Pendennis*, Thackeray condemns himself :

" Even the gentlemen of an age – even these we cannot show as they are, with the notorious selfishness of their age and education. Since the author of *Tom Jones* was buried, no writer of fiction has been permitted to depict to his utmost powers a MAN. We must shape him, give him a certain conventional temper."

So be it. But a man of real literary integrity might have " damned the consequences " and made his own public. A man of worldly wisdom shrugged his shoulders and let his public make him.

In his defence it has been urged that he worked as he did because of an obsession that he must leave his daughters a dowry as big as the patrimony he had wasted. This, too, had its influence upon him, but he earned that dowry more than once, and still he did not change either his way of life or his reckless use of his talent. Except in the case of *Esmond*, he began, after *Vanity Fair*, to regard his work too much as a trade and too little as an art, with the result that we feel in all he wrote a potentiality far greater than its fruits.

After his death, Carlyle said of him : " A beautiful vein of genius lay struggling about in him." It is an apt phrase. His multiplex nature never attained an inward harmony, with the result that in almost all he wrote, there is a straggling, a sense of brilliant vistas sighted and lost again, through lack of power to push on. He stands among the greatest English novelists. He might have stood alone.

The next few years, though full of hard work, were the most enjoyable in Thackeray's life. He had almost everything that his protean nature could want : in London, a comfortable home with two children, now old enough to be companionable ; in Paris, parents too old to be any longer gently tyrannical. In Paris, too, were a better cuisine, cheaper wine and a wider world than that which Dickens dominated ; while in London was a horse, " which," he writes, " I ride in the Park with great elegance. Strange to say, not knowing a horse from a cow, everybody says I have got a most wonderful bargain." Finally, in both London and Paris he had the entrée to that world of fashion which it was so necessary for him to study, if he were to continue satirising it.

Nevertheless, he did not forget old friends, for in *Punch's Prize Novelists*, having scalped Bulwer and Disraeli, he took Charles Lever and put him in the parodist's pillory with " Phil Fogarty " by " Harry Rollicker." That this was only playfulness is evidenced by the fact that, when Lever, previously stirred by *Barry Lyndon*, now came to the boil and wrote furiously to know " what he meant by it," Thackeray was so surprised as to reply in kind. There was the usual sequence of events : an estrangement, and a riposte by Lever in the form of a lampoon of Thackeray in his next novel, *Roland Cashel*. But the greatest tribute the Irish novelist could pay to his tormentor was implicit in the same novel. Lever's style, which Thackeray had so perfectly parodied in " Phil Fogarty," had in *Roland Cashel* completely changed.

With *Vanity Fair* finished and Charles Lever reborn, Thackeray crossed to his cosmopolis with a light heart and a clear conscience. He had been commissioned by Chapman & Hall to write another Christmas book – *The Kickleburys on the Rhine* – had received an advance payment, and with it had removed the last blot from his stepfather's escutcheon by paying off the last instalment of his debt.

But he was beginning to develop that habit of procrastination which filled the chronometrically inspired Trollope with such horror. *The Kickleburys on the Rhine* was so hopelessly in arrears that it was too late for Christmas; while *Pendennis*, which was being written at the time *The Kickleburys* should have been, was made up of "parts" frequently dashed off with the Damoclean printer's boy waiting asleep on a stool. Trollope was hurt by the idea of any man allowing any "part" of a "part-ly" novel to be published till the whole had been written. But Thackeray had not Trollope's tap of inspiration that could be turned on at the signal of an alarm clock. He had, too, been nurtured on hack-journalism, and was still contributing to *Punch* and the *Morning Chronicle*. Moreover, he was periodically attacked by the "blue devils" he so often describes to Mrs. Brookfield, and which were undoubtedly due to the first symptoms of that disease which attacked him with increasing virulence, till it finally killed him.

Indeed, at this time he was so harassed that M. J. Higgins, the famous "Jacob Omnium" of *The Times*, said to him: "If you are tired and want to lie fallow for a year, come to me for the money. I have more than I want."

It was, of course, impossible to accept such an offer. What is less certain is whether Thackeray really needed it. Though he was working hard, he was beginning to live softly. There were some bad tastes to rinse from his mouth, and he rinsed them with good wine. And sometimes he seemed to see the lees at the bottom of the glass, for he wrote to Mrs. Brookfield:

"I don't see that living is such a benefit, and could find it in my heart pretty readily to have an end of it – after wasting a deal of opportunities and time and desires in vanitarianism. What is it makes one so *blasé* and tired, I wonder, at thirty-eight. Is it pain or pleasure?"

The answer is, Both – for he knew both and, to his credit be it said, could hold both without staggering.

In the middle of *Pendennis* he was taken ill, and its publication was suspended for some months. His friends rallied to him, and Mrs. Brookfield so far overcame the decorum of the age as to peep at him in bed, round the edge of the door. He came nearer to dying than he knew, for the illness (a species of cholera) was aggravated and prolonged by the disease of which Mrs. Brookfield wrote to her husband :

" I remember Mr. Thackeray once saying that he had something which prevented his being able to insure his life."

He recovered, and finished *Pendennis*, though he was never satisfied with it. Yet it contained Major Pendennis, a character whom he likened to himself and who was certainly one of the most finished he ever created. But the book as a whole reveals the patchy work of a man who was still half a journalist and could rattle off a digression to fill a " part " as easily as he could an article to fill a column. He was himself so dissatisfied with it that he struck off most of the shackles that still bound him to Grub Street. Only *Punch* remains to remind us, by his outspoken and trenchant articles, how difficult it must have been at times to keep the " organs " in *Pendennis* grinding.

G<small>T</small>

And even then he couldn't please everybody. Captain Shandon and Mr. Bludger were suspiciously like "bright, broken Maginn" and another colleague of the famous but fading days of the *Fraserians*. And there was still a kick left in the " old gang." He was accused of " fostering a baneful prejudice against literary men and condescending to caricature (as is too often his habit) his literary fellow-labourers in order to pay court to the non-literary class."

Was there not something a little presumptive in that phrase " literary fellow-labourers " ? Could a man never outgrow his youthful follies, even when he was the rival of Dickens in literature and the " lion of the gay " in " Vanity Fair " ? But was there not also something a little pathetic in the cry of old comrades who had shared old hardships ?

He replied gently : " My attempt was to tell the truth, and I meant it not unkindly."

On the whole, his defence stands. His picture of Captain Shandon is not unsympathetic, though it is distinctly unjust, and in Bludger is depicted a type not pleasant enough in real life to suffer much from caricature in fiction. Regretfully we must admit that, had Thackeray declined to use such promising material, we might have admired him more as a man, but certainly less as a novelist. He probably thought the same.

But, motive and decorum apart, there is something curiously apposite in this criticism of the erstwhile critic by his erstwhile colleagues. The past is behind him. Bulwer-baiting is over.

Gin-and-water has given place to claret, and the table at the Cyder Cellars is emptied of another figure, who has followed "bright, broken Maginn" away from cups and colleagues – not to the Fleet, but on into the endless highways and byways of Vanity Fair.

And the cry from "literary fellow-labourers" sounds both as the malediction and valediction of Grub Street to its most truculent recruit who, after years of seasoned service, is promoted from the rank and file to a commission among rank and fashion.

He had outdistanced Bulwer and Ainsworth ; was on a level with Dickens ; his "songs were being sung in the streets," and in the drawing-room his tall, broad figure moved with elegance and dignity. Swashbuckling days were over, and ahead lay the "pavement sermons" of *The Roundabout Papers*.

As though to signalise his apotheosis, his hair had turned quite white.

CHAPTER VII

The English Humourists – quarrel with the Brookfields – *Esmond* commissioned – differences with and resignation from *Punch* – sails for America.

THACKERAY was a notoriously bad speaker. On the rare occasions when he completed what he had to say, it was to discover afterwards that he had not said what he meant. With such a disconcerting handicap, it must have required considerable courage to contemplate giving a series of lectures. But Thackeray always had courage, and, at this time, anxiety. If he did not gather all the fruits of success while they were within his grasp, he might fail to leave that dowry for his daughters, to which he refers perhaps a little too often. Dickens was regularly giving public readings of his works and had made a fortune by lecturing in America. It was an example worth following, and Thackeray followed it. *The English Humourists* had been written principally in Paris, in the intervals of a "lionisation" equal to any that he had received in England. At a ball given by Lady Sandwich he had met and impressed Lord Castlereagh. With previous meetings with Lord Melbourne and Sir Robert Peel, this meant that, not content with associating with the aristocracy, he had collected the "tufts" of no less than three Prime Ministers. He was later to add a fourth in Lord Palmerston. Of course he was called a sycophant, but somehow Lord Palmerston seems to justify him. For Palmerston was an unusual man. He had English common sense, a strain of Gallic realism, an urbane humour and a nonchalance that had its origin in the preceding century. Between such a man and the author of *Vanity Fair* there was much in common, more, perhaps, than Thackeray found between himself and the circles who called " all his good people fools and all his clever ones knaves." Palmerston probably said the same, and, if he did, Thackeray probably agreed, with the added possibility that, having agreèd, they both laughed and opened another bottle of claret.

Indeed, such people as Palmerston and his circle would require from a guest something more than the simple arts of the " tuft-hunter." Their hospitality may have been the last flicker of the " patronage " which distinguished the preceding century, but it was also the last testimony of that age to the man who most nearly expressed its fading elegance. For the author of *Vanity Fair* was something more than a novelist or a satirist. He was a personage, and to his lectures came the last line of those who were guiding England through her transition from an aristocratic to a middle-class ethic.

The omens were good. The season was opportune, the nation optimistic. Three weeks earlier, Prince Albert, having previously decided that universal peace had arrived and that the millennium was approaching, had determined to commemorate the double event by opening the Great Exhibition. Thackeray's opinion of the Great Exhibition may be found in *Punch* of May 1851, but he had never seen eye to eye with Prince Albert, whom he had once called Queen Victoria's "poor dear gentlewoman." Nevertheless, he owed a good deal to the Prince Consort's Exhibition. In the gay season that opened with the dawn of a universal peace, Thackeray's lectures ultimately became the mood of the modish.

To the first, at Willis' Rooms, flocked a sprinkling of the *ton* and the cream of the intelligentsia – Ladies Waldegrave and Molesworth, the Lord Chief Baron and Sir Robert Peel, Macaulay and Dean Millman, Lady Ashburton with her set, Mrs. Proctor with her *salon* and Mrs. Brookfield with her circle. Carlyle also had loyally left his tub, though he had found a new cause for gloom in the regrettable tendency of literary men to lecture. As leaven, came the *Punch* contingent, with one member master of a set of signals which Thackeray would give him from the platform, when applause or emotion were needed.

Standing " off " was Thackeray himself, bathed in the luminous perspiration of stage-fright. But his anxiety was unnecessary. The lectures were a brilliant success, not only in their matter, but in the manner of their delivery, which one of the audience described as that of " an educated gentleman reading to an educated assembly." Punctuated by educated applause, the " soft, deep, sonorous " voice read on to a triumphant conclusion.

But in one sense it was a Pyrrhic victory. Most of the seats were free. This was remedied subsequently, and the lectures became one of the fashionable events of the season. Currer Bell, now openly avowing herself as Charlotte Brontë, attended one " composed of the *élite* of London, with duchesses by the score," as she rather fretfully wrote in describing the Vain success of the author of *Vanity Fair*, so recently described by her in her dedication as the " first social regenerator of his day."

It was stated that he made nearly four thousand pounds by the lectures, but the information came from Charlotte Brontë, who was always prone to exaggerate the " worldly " success of a man who had become rather a disappointment to her. But, whatever he made in money, he made a name as " the greatest satirist of the age."

A well-earned holiday on the Rhine with his children was his immediate indulgence, and when he returned it was to repeat his lectures and success in Scotland. But before this tour he virtually lost his " dear lady," for on his return from the Rhine he quarrelled with her husband.

The Rev. Brookfield was ill, and in the peevishness of illness was harsh in speech to his wife in the presence of Thackeray. The latter replied in terms which later, when cooler, he admitted to be " quite unjustifiable." The rupture was violent, but apparently there were no accusations. Indeed, the breach was healed by the husband a while later, and the letters between Thackeray and Mrs. Brookfield resumed. Nevertheless, there had been, at least on Thackeray's side, some sort of protestations, though how much we can read into them depends on the extent to which we find convincing the hyperbole which distinguishes most declarations of an emotional or moral character during the 'forties. In two letters he mentions his love for her, but he also couples with it his love for her husband, which, though it adds to their propriety, detracts from their poignancy. Further, to the more impassioned of these she had replied :

" Do you know that, if you do not write in more commonplace style to me, I shall be quite unable to answer at all."

This circumspect answer had produced a bitter retort, in which he asks whether he shall begin to call her " Mrs. Brookfield " again.

His real feelings are best gauged by reading his customary letters to her, through which runs an undertone of real tenderness, half-hidden by whimsicality and muted by a playfully sardonic note. After the rupture such letters were never written again, though he corresponded with her during his American tour. It is his letters to Kate Perry which show that his " queer, uncouth raptures " had developed into something deeper – deeper, perhaps, than his " dear lady " quite expected.

But two years later his mood has changed, and he writes to his mother :

" We have seen the poor Brookfields, and the moral I have come to is, ' Thou shalt not pity thy neighbour's wife. Keep out of his harem, it is better for you and for him.' "

This is not the note of a broken heart, slowly healed by time. And so soon he was to write *The Newcomes*, in which he turns and rends his old friend, W. H. Brookfield, in the character of the Rev. Honeyman.

Altogether it is a mysterious love-affair, unless we look at Elizabeth in *Lovel the Widower* – a girl whom more than one man loved, and one of whose admirers is named by Thackeray, in italics, as " William," as Mrs. Brookfield's husband was. And there are cryptic references to Elizabeth's laughter at a man with white hair, whom she never regarded in any other way save as an *uncle*. And a riposte, so reminiscent of other injuries received and repaid :

" Passionate outbursts of a grief-stricken heart ! – Passionate scrapings of a fiddle-stick, my good friend. . . . Despair is perfectly compatible with a good dinner, I promise you. Hair is false ; hearts are false. Grapes may be sour, but claret is good, my masters."

And from Mrs. Brookfield we hear nothing. There is only a collection of letters that " redound to the credit of all parties concerned."

So his " dear lady " passes out of his life, though her own continues serenely as she moves on, back still straight from the " back-board," to bear her husband children, read his facetious letters, discuss the " news " of Thackeray's death, write a novel or two of indifferent quality, and smile, in later years, gently at Kate Perry, who affirms that, of all the women friends poor Mr. Thackeray had, she, his " dear lady," was the most cherished.

But these events were distant, and in the present his anodynes were the lectures and *Esmond*. George Smith had commissioned the book, on the comfortable terms of £1,200 for a first edition of 2,500 copies and half profits on receipts above that figure.

Thackeray had further grounds for self-congratulation. The novel was not to be published in " parts," and for the first time he was free to devote his over-occupied brain to the production of its purest fruit. But even with circumstances so favourable he was behindhand with the novel and would have liked another six months in which to polish it. Nevertheless, when it was finally published he said of it, " Here is the very best that I can do. I stand by this book, and am willing to leave it when I go, as my card."

And his card it remains, in its elegant eighteenth-century prose with its great historical figures, Marlborough, the Young Pretender, the wits, Addison and Steele ; its duelling and dicing, the bright treachery of politicians and their placemen ; and Beatrix Esmond, the one and only rival to Becky Sharp, and one of the most superbly drawn characters in English fiction.

With that " card," Thackeray could gain the entrée to any society in any age, and yet – if beyond he sought admittance to the shadowy company of Le Sage, Molière, Fielding and Sterne, he would need to carry beneath his arm the " yellow-backed " volumes of *Vanity Fair*, and enter eternity as the Master Showman of his century.

Indeed *Esmond* had only two blemishes, and Thackeray labelled one himself. Esmond was a prig, he said, omitting to add that Lady Castlewood was in the best tradition of the nineteenth-century Madonnas of the Bustle.

But before it was published he had written *The English Humourists of the Eighteenth Century* and was planning a voyage to America to reap such a golden harvest as had awaited Dickens. Before he went he removed the last traces of his life in the " ranks " by resigning from *Punch*.

Financial worries were over and the " organs were grinding his tunes." Moreover, fashion and intelligence were flocking to his lectures and *Esmond* was soo to be printed as his card. He had no need to cherish sentimental regrets. He and the little humpbacked geni had met at the right time and made each other famous. Each could now stand alone, and he decided that it were best they should. For *Punch* was developing dangerous views, or he was cultivating more circumspect ones.

He had tried to effect the rupture earlier, when, suspecting Jerrold of an ultra-republican article, he had told Mrs. Brookfield that he " could not pull any longer in the same boat with such a savage little Robespierre." But Jerrold was not guilty; and whoever was, was suppressed, together with his " sea-green " views, leaving Thackeray no alternative but to remain on *Punch's* " Committee of Public Safety." Nevertheless, water was flowing rapidly beneath the bridge of " the first social regenerator of his day." When he finally resigned he gave as reasons " serious public differences with the conduct of *Punch* — about the abuse of Prince Albert and the Crystal Palace at wh. I very nearly resigned, about abuse of Lord Palmerston, about abuse finally of Louis Napoleon."

His sponsorship of Prince Albert is puzzling, for he had never admired him as a man and was never prepared to admire any man merely because he was a king, a prince or a consort. His robust republicanism had more than once satirised the " royalty-worship " of his contemporaries. The Crystal Palace, too, had never attracted him, and, again, he had used *Punch* as the vehicle for expressing a contempt for the Exhibition hardly less than that he had shown for the plaster and tinsel pageantry of the Second Funeral of Napoleon. Lord Palmerston was a different matter. Thackeray had earlier been called to the Bar, with the hope of a police-magistracy to relieve the financial strain of writing. And, later, he wrote to his mother :

" I think it possible that Lord Palmerston will ask me to dinner on Saturday, wh. I don't choose to refuse him again : I was obliged to last week, being engaged to Tennent. And he is the man who has Police Magistrateships in his gift. O ! thou schemer and artful dodger ! "

Such sly candour is disarming, and at least he stood by Palmerston over Louis Napoleon, though even in that it is difficult to decide whether it was because he liked Palmerston or because he disliked Louis Philippe. He had scarified Louis

Philippe so often, and just before resigning from *Punch* had written in his very best vein a denunciation of the king who ran away from his throne. When the exiled monarch had become a " special constable " and Louis Napoleon had taken his vacant throne, Thackeray perhaps felt again that preference for the knave over the fool, even when the knave celebrated his *coup d'état* by a *battue* in the streets of Paris, reminiscent of his grandfather's robust and salutary " whiff of grapeshot."

But in any case his hair was white now, and the red cap of Liberty would look outlandish on a head of white hair. And had not his old friend, Fitz, rung out sweet music from the Persian lyre ? —

Ah ! take the Cash in hand and waive the Rest.
Oh ! the brave music of a distant *Drum !*

So he resigned, though he still retained the little silver statuette of *Punch* presented to him by a number of admirers when he first became famous as the author of *The Book of Snobs*. *Honoris causa* — but honour was satisfied. The statuette he retained till the end of his life — a sentimental symbol of less prosperous days, when Greenwich and the Bedford had seen the weekly " Cabinet " attended by a number of jovial, hard-working, hard-hitting friends, who had, nevertheless, shown some softness of heart towards the Fat Contributor.

For their sakes, or perhaps for his own, he continued after his resignation to attend the weekly meeting, till in later life when, though his place was always laid, it was never filled.

Meanwhile, he was free at last – free of *Fraser's*, free of the Cyder Cellars, free of the little gentleman with a hump who, nevertheless, continued in silver effigy to grin slyly at him ; so impudent, so cynical, so republican and so inconvenient. But there is " a tide in the affairs of men which, taken at the flood, leads on to fortune." For an instant we see him, sitting in his chair with the little statuette in front of him. Then he rises, smiles and bows, rings for his secretary and his valet, and steps out into the " great club of the world " to take ship for a newer land where the sun shines upon the booths of a newer and bigger Fair.

And the New World awaited him, for already Carlyle had written to Emerson : " Item : Thackeray ; who is coming over to lecture to you : a mad world, my Masters ! "

CHAPTER VIII

The first American tour – ill health – The Newcomes – The Four Georges and the second American tour – stands for Parliament at Oxford and is defeated – The Virginians.

THE success of the tour was inevitable. Not only was *The English Humourists of the Eighteenth Century* a model of what the " spoken " essay should be, but it was spoken by a famous and fashionable man to a people still callow enough to be conscious of their pioneer past and earnest enough to seek in English literature, not only its intrinsic qualities, but the cachet that Old World culture would confer upon New World wealth.

Their own Washington Irving had already, in his *Sketch Books*, drawn a picture of English life and manners completely convincing to those who had never experienced either, while Prescott had gone to Spain to find in hidalgo and morrisco the heroic and noble ancestors of a nation which had been born free and snobless.

And there were other influences at work to ensure that Thackeray had a favourable reception. America was still smarting from *Martin Chuzzlewit* and Dickens' lofty but tactless reactions to American slavery.

In the person of Thackeray, the New World saw a trenchant satirist from the Old, who, judging by his *Irish* and *Paris Sketch Books*, would probably be quite capable of writing an "American" replica. If Dickens could turn moral indignation into a more saleable commodity, what had they not to fear from one who, in addition to being moral, was satirical?

But if the hosts were anxious to please, the guest was just as anxious to appease. He had several reasons.

"What could Dickens mean," he writes to Fonblanque, " by writing that book of American notes. No man should write about the country under five years experience."

And to his mother : " Shall I make a good bit of money in America and write a book about it? I think not. It seems impudent to write a book, and mere sketches are somehow below my rank in the world – I mean, a grave old gentleman, father of young ladies, mustn't be comic and grinning too much."

His third letter was to Kate Perry, after the tour had begun to " rain dollars " :

" I don't intend to make a book. No, no. The goose is much too good a goosey to be killed. In fact, I'm looking ahead."

He was – three years ahead, when he gave his second and even more lucrative lectures to the New World. And from the very outset the " golden goosey " cackled earnestly and laid faithfully. His first lecture in New York was a greater triumph than that in Willis' Rooms. For not only were all the seats paid for, but in place of *Fraser's* reporters were those from the *New York Evening Post*, who thus reported him and his lecture:

"His hair appears to have kept silvery record over fifty years; and then there was a notion in the minds of many that there must be something dashing and 'fast' in his appearance, whereas his costume was perfectly plain, the expression of his face grave and earnest, his address perfectly unaffected. . . . His voice is superb tenor and possesses that pathetic tremble which is so effective in what is called emotive eloquence."

How could any "goosey" refuse to lay her golden tribute at the feet of such a man? But if the American reporter was more polite than *Fraser's*, he was quite as critical, for he added:

"There has been nothing written about Swift so clever, and, if we except Lord Orrery's silly letters, we suspect we may add, nothing so unjust. Though suitable credit was given to Swift's talents, all of which were admirably characterised, yet when he came to speak of the moral side of the Dean's nature, he saw nothing but darkness."

But though here and there a critic might cavil, his progress was a triumph and his reception by the American people as big a tribute to their hearts as the popularity of his essay was to their heads.

It is curious to see the effect of so new a civilisation upon a man so essentially the product of an older world.

"It's the most curious varnish of a Civilisation," he writes to a friend. "The girls are all dressed like the most stunning French actresses, the houses furnished like the most splendid gambling-houses." And to Mrs. Brookfield he confesses : " The rush and restlessness please me. I like for a little the dash of the stream." He also mentions that " the jolly manner answers here very well, which I have from Nature or Art possibly."

Indeed, we must always regret that the " golden goosey " prevented his writing that " American Sketch Book," for vivid descriptions of peoples, customs and manners were among Thackeray's greatest attributes as a writer. Sufficiently gregarious to absorb temporarily the emotions and moods of those about him, he was never completely submerged by the enthusiasms of others – nor, indeed, by his own. He skims the cream off all the human milk he samples and pours it into a cup for us to drink. It is a rich cup, but not a deep one.

His letters, during both his tours, supply in part the missing " Sketch Book." He gives a picture of a warm-hearted, jostling, self-conscious people ; half humble, half defiant towards the great white-haired " gentleman " from the Western World. And his response is half jocular, half bored, but wholly practical.

At Boston he lectured to nearly twelve hundred people, having left at New York " near a thousand pounds, which Baring's house will invest for me, so that my girls will be very considerably the better for the journey."

He met Washington Irving, Prescott, Longfellow, Oliver Wendell Holmes, and enjoyed their company as they did his. But, though he found "the jolly manner answer very well," we see him, through the eyes of R. H. Dana, courteous, but not too talkative.

"Thackeray is not a great talker," observes Dana. "He was interested in all that was said, and put in a pleasant word occasionally."

Attentive, but faintly aloof, the satirist sits and listens to the gay earnestness of a younger world, but when his popularity in Philadelphia leads the most prominent citizens to ask him to apply for the post of British Consul, he expresses his gratification but pleads the call of " the familiar London flagstone and the library at the Athenæum, and the ride in the Park and the pleasant society afterwards."

America might be the home of the " golden goosey," but Major Pendennis begins to want his club and the Mall again. And America was so different from the Mall. In letters sent to his daughters on his second tour, he drew sketches of a row of people in the train, all eating with their knives, and wrote lugubriously : " The dreariness of this country [Alabama] everywhere almost consumes me . . . the stink, the dirt, the foul glasses, the dingy shirts (many of them with grand diamond brooches making a sunshine in those shady places), the peeps of flannel, the hands and the nails."

Not even the homes of Prescott, Irving and Longfellow could compensate him, though he describes them as " comfortable old houses, handsome, large libraries, and famous Burgundy and Claret in their cellars."

But the negroes awake a flash of old moods, and he writes:

"The negroes don't shock me or excite my compassionate feelings at all, they are so grotesquely happy that I can't cry over them."

This is in marked contrast with Dickens, who insisted on crying over them; not because they were unhappy, but because, as slaves, they ought to be.

With "Sam" Wilberforce in charge of the national conscience, it was perhaps imprudent of Thackeray to write:

"Of course we feel the cruelty of flogging and enslaving a negro – of course they feel the cruelty of starving an English labourer or of driving an English child into a mine – Brother! Brother! we are kin."

But this was in a private letter. It was not in *Punch*, as it might have been a few years earlier. Nevertheless, even if it cannot be used to support his claim as a public moralist, it is definite evidence of his private honesty. Indeed, the candour of his letters frequently discounts the charges of hypocrisy made against him. Humbug he frequently was, and had to be, but he seldom deceived himself, except when his dignity was touched, and never tried to deceive those who knew him intimately. Those who did not must form their own opinion with such little aids as discretion might suggest to him. And at that time ill health must often have prompted him to discretion. So frequently he had to leave both lecture-room and dining-table and in the privacy of his bedroom, abandon in agony " the jolly manner that answered so well." Perhaps it was some such mood that suddenly led him to cut short his tour and return post-haste to England, to hurry off, on his first day back in London, to a ball that was being given that night by Lady Stanley of Alderley. The next few days, too, saw him feverishly renewing old contacts, revisiting all his old clubs, old hosts and old associates, before setting off more leisurely to join his daughters on the Continent and to listen to them playing Haydn and Mozart on the piano.

Those who are more interested in a good man than in a good writer may wish that he had listened to Haydn and Mozart first and visited Lady Stanley and his clubs later. But he was in the difficult position of having to satisfy simultaneously the often conflicting claims of the fashionable novelist, the confirmed epicurean, the dutiful son and the devoted father. He referred at this time to " the funny little world my old folks live in," and Mrs. Browning, who met him with his daughters in Rome, stated that " Mr. Thackeray ... complains of dullness – he is disabled from work by dullness. He ' can't write in the morning without his good dinner and two parties overnight.' From such a soil spring the *Vanity Fairs* ! "

But Mrs. Browning did not like him, and few of his contemporaries understood him.

A man must not make money to spend it, nor seek good company for pleasure, nor have children for affection. Money must be saved, associates must be elevating and children must be improved. He did his best. His eldest daughter, Anne, became his amanuensis during the writing of *The Newcomes*, and both she and her sister his companions when circumstances permitted. For the rest, he left them their dowries and gained their affections, so perhaps we may forgive him if he spent his money and liked " his two parties overnight."

Certainly the parties gave him no more " copy," for never again did his art produce an *Esmond* nor his genius a *Vanity Fair*.

" Never mind," he wrote of *The Newcomes* ; this is not written for glory, but for quite as good an object, namely, money, which will profit the children more than reputation, when there's an end of me."

And there were not only his own two girls to think of, but Amy Crowe, daughter of an old friend, whom he had adopted – a practical example of kindness that goes further than the customary and florid declarations of affection that were so essential in his day if a man wished to be recognised as a good father as well as a good writer.

Indeed, at this time, his is a difficult character to fit into the niche of biographical tradition. Though he had everything that a biographer could wish him – money, fame, friends and family – yet somehow he remains a rather lonely figure. We " hear " of him more than we " see " of him. He is at a tavern dinner with Leech and Maclise, at a literary centenary with Foster and

Dickens, drops in at the Procters' and chats awhile. But in the lives and memoirs of his contemporaries he is rather a shadowy figure, seen often, but not for long. Fitzgerald leaves his " bowl of wine and book of verse " for a last dinner with his old friend, which over, he says grace with the words : " He wouldn't come again, as everyone had had enough of Fitz."

Harrison Ainsworth reappears at the invitation of the man who had parodied him in unsuccessful days and now dines him in the unrelenting present, which had left Ainsworth's reputation in the past and was filling all England with his host's fame.

Thackeray has been accused of patronising in success those who had helped him in adversity. But it is an unsubtle charge. For both in success and failure Thackeray's character remained the same. And vanity was no small part of it. In failure, vanity produced resentment ; in success, kindliness ; and in both, its essential quality – attention to himself. It is probable that in entertaining Ainsworth he wished his quondam rival to see his success, but he wished it, not to make Ainsworth conscious of his own past fame, but dazzlingly aware of his host's present fortunes. Similarly, he wrote a review of Cruickshank's work, when Cruickshank, too, was in the wake of his fortune's ship. For Cruickshank had had the pick of illustrating in the days when Thackeray still thought himself an artist. It was kindliness, prompted by egotism, but it was kindliness, just the same. There was probably a little dignity too. Wealth and fame brought obligations, and he fulfilled them. " Noblesse oblige – mais toujours la noblesse."

The Newcomes was a success. It was nearer Dickens in spirit than anything Thackeray had written, and its " parts " were read with almost the same eagerness. In its descriptions of the *beau monde* it nearly re-creates the world of Rawdon Crawley and the little demi-rep, Becky Sharp. But the gay irony is replaced by a fretful moralising, and Clive and his father exhibit a noble peevishness in the world of the parvenu and among the beautiful merchandise of the Marriage Market. In Lady Kew and Ethel Newcome are two characters who might have stepped out of *Vanity Fair*. But Lady Kew dies early and Ethel is purified by suffering till she is indistinguishable from Laura Pendennis. There remains only Colonel Newcome, who unfortunately remains to the end.

But perhaps Thackeray knew his faults. For he called Colonel Newcome " rather a twaddler " later, and as soon as the book was published turned to the eighteenth century again.

For a while he lies hidden, busily writing, to re-emerge with *The Four Georges* tucked under his arm, and a passage booked for America.

America was mad to see " the author of *The Newcomes*," even if he had nothing better to talk to them about than the coarse, profligate eighteenth century.

His valet laconically notes in his diary : " The lecture was too smutty for the fair sex." Success was for a moment in doubt. The New World was a little uneasy about "George I and his strumpets." But, as the strumpets were English and the King a George, America succumbed, particularly to the lecture on George III, "because of the pathetic business," and the second tour was even more successful than the first. The Georges, their strumpets and pathos, and "a beautiful tribute of loyalty to Queen Victoria and the tone and manners of her Court" yielded in America and England combined another dowry for his daughters, totalling £20,000.

"It is as much as I want," he writes to a friend; "10,000 apiece for the girls is enough for any author's daughters."

But "George's strumpets" gave offence in England. No loyal man should accuse a King of carnal appetites, particularly when the King is related dynastically to the reigning Queen. Fortunately, Thackeray could quote the "beautiful tribute of loyalty to Queen Victoria." But it was a timely reminder that he lived in the nineteenth and not in the eighteenth century. He remembered, and though he trespassed once more in *The Virginians*, it was a half-hearted sequel to its splendid forerunner, *Esmond*, and reflected the tastes of his public more nearly than that of its period.

His health led him once again to toy with the idea of a police-magistracy. On the whole, his failure to obtain one is fortunate. Some years earlier, Titmarsh on the Bench might have added a brighter note to British justice. But the author of *The Newcomes*, who had been forbidden to talk of royal strumpets, would probably have fallen back on legal moralising, a combination which, from the criminal's point of view, adds insult to injury.

Failing to obtain the police-magistracy, he decided to enter Parliament. He had precedent to support him, for both Bulwer and Disraeli had combined a political with a literary career. Whether their example influenced him we do not know. Throughout his life he had been prone to emulate any man who was doing anything that he thought he could do as well or better himself. In this, as in so many other of his actions, we must look for more than one motive. Though he had negatived the Philadelphians' suggestion that he should apply for a consulship, he had written letters at the time to friends, which show that he was flattered by the idea. And to Mrs. Brookfield he had confided while in America that, when he had given his second tour and earned his daughters their dowry, he might try other things than writing.

"There is money-making to try at," he wrote "and ambition – I mean public life, perhaps that might interest a man, but not novels nor lectures nor fun any more."

He may have felt that a Parliamentary career was the obligation of a man who had succeeded in the more pressing ventures of life. He may even have thought that there was room among the Whigs for the trenchant republican who had written for *Punch*. It is also not improbable that he fancied the cachet that a seat in Parliament would give to a man already so famous in the literary and fashionable world. So often we see him thus looking at himself, in some new mirror of his own fashioning – dramatising himself, watching his own progress from obscurity to fame.

But this last dignity was denied him. Though he selected Oxford as his constituency, Oxford selected his opponent and he was left with the civic honour of paying a thousand pounds for his efforts. It was paid almost entirely in silver dollars.

Following the election, he was again ill, and *The Virginians*, commissioned by Bradbury & Evans a year earlier, did not blossom into its first " part " till the October of 1857. Three hundred pounds per number was the amount paid for a book made up of " pot-boiling " to keep up to date with the " parts," garrulity to keep in touch with the public, history to remind himself of what he might have done if he had husbanded instead of gambling with his gifts, and sluggishness to mark the mental and physical condition of the man who, for some years now, had been living a " liberal, costly," but no longer " a lazy " life.

" Claret drunk not wisely but too well," he wrote to a friend, " an immoderate use of the flesh-pots, are beginning to tell."

It says something for the courage and nonchalance of this protean man, that he could name the contributory and conceal the real cause of the premature sluggishness of so supple a mind. Only at times comes a whimsical cry *de profundis*, as when he could write of the toils of composing *The Virginians* :

"A fit of spasms – then get well in about five days, then five days grumbling and thinking of my work, then fourteen days work and spasms *da capo* – and what a horribly stupid story I am writing. . . . No incident, no character, no go left in this dreary old expiring carcase."

He was then forty-seven years of age.

CHAPTER IX

The Yates affair – quarrel with Dickens – opinions on *The Virginians* – the editorship of the *Cornhill* – relations with Trollope – increasing illness – *Lovel the Widower* and *Philip* – back to the eighteenth century with *Denis Duval* – the last quarrel – death.

AT the height of his success, Thackeray received an unpleasant reminder of past exuberances. One Yates, a journalist of small repute and less manners, but a fellow-member of the Garrick Club, contributed to *Town Talk* an article on Thackeray, his work, career and, of course, his appearance. The "broken nose" comes in again, set in a "bloodless," and "not particularly expressive" face. His bearing is "cold and uninviting, his style of conversation either openly cynical or affectedly good-natured and benevolent; his *bonhomie* is forced, his wit biting, his pride easily touched – but his appearance is invariably that of the cool, *suave*, well-bred gentleman, who, whatever may be rankling within, suffers no surface display of his emotions."

Appearances were deceptive, for "whatever was rankling within" did suffer a very marked "surface display." The "cool, *suave*, well-bred gentleman" did not, as Pope would have done, ignore or merely "cane" the man; he began by demanding an apology and, not receiving it, ended by demanding Yates' expulsion from the club.

On the committee that was formed to examine the charges was Dickens, for whom Yates worked on the staff of *Household Words*. The committee decided, with Dickens as the single dissentient, that Yates must go. He went, leaving behind him a silence between Thackeray and Dickens, which he advertised with his tongue and capitalised in a book.

Thackeray's case was that Yates had committed a breach of manners in violating the confidence of club membership, and a breach of taste in attacking, not the quality of his written work, but the motives that inspired it. And on both counts he had justice on his side, for Yates in the article made use of private conversation overheard in the club, and in his criticism of Thackeray's work made the charge that "no one succeeds better than Mr. Thackeray in cutting his coat according to his cloth. Here he followed the aristocracy; but when he crossed the Atlantic, George Washington became the idol of his worship, the 'Four Georges' the object of his bitterest attacks."

The charge was, of course, unfounded, for Thackeray had given both lectures – *The English Humourists* and *The Four Georges* – in both England and America. Indeed, in giving *The Four Georges* in England he had also given offence, for he had written:

"The big-wigs and great folks are furious. The halls of splendour are closed to me. . . . Shall I ever write a book again? Some day, please God, when these astonishing Georges have put a few thousands more into my pocket."

To be called a sycophant when he had so boldly given offence, was perhaps one reason why he took it.

Dickens, in voting against Yates' expulsion, has been accused of malice against Thackeray, but no adequate motive for malice has been adduced. The more probable explanation is that Yates being a colleague of Dickens, and Dickens being a man of great kindness to colleagues, the latter felt that, as between kindness and manners, he was as much entitled to his preferences as Thackeray was to his. He probably also felt the additional difficulty that Yates had only done to one fellow-member what Thackeray had done to another. For no special pleading can make any essential distinction between the taste that led Yates to lampoon Thackeray, and Thackeray to lampoon, as Foker in *Pendennis*, Archdeckne, a fellow-member of the Garrick. True, there was a difference in manners, for Thackeray's parody was clever, if cruel and disguised, if recognisable, while Yates' was neither clever nor cruel nor veiled. It was merely impertinent, and, which was worse, reminiscent of similar reviewing by Thackeray in his *Fraserian* days.

That Yates deserved neither Dickens' kindness nor Thackeray's manners is the more regrettable, since, despite his smallness, he was large enough to stand between two men so much bigger than himself. They were not reconciled till the last year of Thackeray's life.

No one gained anything except the club –

which lost Yates. For Dickens was accused of malice, and Thackeray, though his dignity was vindicated by crossing swords with a mud-lark, was reminded that before he took to the sword he had thrown mud himself.

While *The Virginians* was still being pumped and shovelled into the fortnightly moulds, John Blackwood expressed the view that " he must improve much or the book will not keep up his reputation." Thackeray himself admitted as much : " I dawdled fatally between parts V. and X. . . . I am old, or I am tired, or some other reason."

If he could not determine, who can ? Illness certainly played the larger part, but he hints at other causes when he writes :

" We give very good dinners, our house is full of pretty little things, our cellar is not badly off. . . . I am going in a few days to pay £100 for eighteen dozen of '48 claret that is not to be drunk for four years."

He also kept an open carriage and a brougham, and his daughters had good masters for the best lessons – music, drawing, dancing and riding.

He was certainly an indulgent father, but he was forgetful. The two dowries of £10,000 were being spent before he was dead or his daughters were married.

Fortunately, the benevolent George Smith had been watching this elderly " rake's progress," and now stepped in with an offer of a salary of £350 per month to Thackeray, if he would work exclusively for the firm and assign to them the exclusive rights of publication, both serially in the magazine which Smith was about to launch, and in volume form when completed. It was not a police-magistracy, but it was a salary, and one that would have corrupted any magistrate. Thackeray accepted graciously. The next item was an editor for the magazine. After cogitation, Smith decided that if he kept control he might do worse than have so famous a man as Thackeray for the nominal editor. Who would not wish to contribute to and read a first-class periodical presided over by a novelist who rivalled Dickens, and a satirist whose most dangerous fangs had been drawn? He offered the post to Thackeray with a salary of £1,000 a year, over and above the £350 per month already agreed on.

Thackeray raised his eyes to heaven, and accepted, christening the magazine the *Cornhill*. It was to contain contributions "from lettered and instructed men" on all permissible subjects, but no " party politics " and no " sectarianism." Finally, the moral tone was to make the magazine suitable for family consumption. His own contributions were *The Roundabout Papers*, which he calls his " pavement sermons," while Lady Ritchie writes : " Working in his own line, a week-day preacher as he loved to call himself, he takes peaceful iteration of daily duty for his text and preaches the supremacy of goodness."

From a truculent shaveling of *Fraser's* to the editorship of a magazine that preached " the supremacy of goodness " was a long journey. But he arrived – almost. Now and again in *The*
It

Roundabout Papers he forgets himself and hits hard at some of the old phantoms – at snobs, and at Louis Philippe, and once, really hard, at America when it threatened to impound British stocks in the event of war; but on the whole the papers are "pavement sermons"; pleasant trifles, suitable for family consumption; suave, but no longer ironic; moral, but no longer satirical.

As he sits in his editorial chair what passes behind those inscrutable, spectacled eyes, so benevolent in late years, so combative before the hair had turned white? Perhaps he draws little sketches on the virgin paper waiting to be filled – sketches of men in tye-wigs and periwigs, with rapiers and canes; little pen-and-ink ghosts of dead gallants, gamblers and wits, limned idly on the paper that is waiting to be filled with a message for middle-class England.

Well, well, for twenty years he had spoken his mind, and always they had asked him to speak theirs. In his journeyings in Vanity Fair he had too often struggled through the Slough of Despond not to emerge finally as Mr. Worldly Wiseman. "All his good people had been fools, and all his clever ones knaves." And had he not written in a letter to a friend: "What care I to appear to future ages (who will be deeply interested in discussing the subject) as other than I really am?"

And he was then white-haired, with two charming daughters and a comfortable home; he was also older than his years and tired, rather tired, and ill – more ill than any of them knew. "Let us eat, drink and be moral, for to-morrow we ..."

The sales of the *Cornhill* were "staggering." The first issue sold 120,000 copies. The subtle but benevolent Smith promptly doubled the stipend of his lay-preacher, who wrote excitedly :

"We've got two horses in our carriage now. The magazine goes on selling, and how much do you think my next twelve months' earnings and receipts will be, if I work? £10,000 ! Cockadoodleodoodle !"

He received, in addition to his stipend, twelve guineas per page for his "sermons." Hurriedly he wrote to share his good fortune with his friends, soliciting contributions from Tennyson, Carlyle and Augustus Sala. All thanked him, but only Sala contributed. Carlyle was too busy with *Frederick the Great*, and Tennyson had given his only suitable poem to a rival magazine. But the poet was glad to hear from "my old friend," though he added, rather unkindly to one who was composing "pavement sermons" : "You have engaged for any quantity of money to let your brains be sucked periodically by Smith Elder & Co."

As a "lay preacher," Thackeray turned the other cheek – this time to Trollope, whom he asked, rather appropriately, to contribute one of his clerical stories. Trollope seems to have misunderstood him, for he sent one which he admits himself, in his *Life of Thackeray*, was rather naughty, "because therein a gentleman contemplated running away with a married lady !"

Perhaps he thought that as the gentleman only contemplated the abduction, it might pass. But Thackeray shook his head indulgently. A clever fellow, Trollope, but almost as salacious as Charles Reade. " *Virginibus puerisque,*" he replied regretfully. Trollope quite understood and supplied an alternative.

Thackeray as an editor was not very successful. He was always unbusinesslike and always fretful of restraint. He had another fatal weakness in an editor : he felt pity for his contributors, especially those whose outpourings were unsuitable for publication. So often they were accompanied by such pitiful letters as the one he quotes in his editorial sermon, *Pins in the Cushion.* Surreptitious five-pound notes found their way with the rejection slips to those who needed money as badly as he had done, and, for that matter, still did. For he was frequently in the habit of signifying to the ubiquitous and accommodating Smith that times were temporarily bad, by walking into his room with his trousers pockets turned inside out.

So we see him in glimpses – in his editorial chair, or with his daughters driving at dusk through the Park in the carriage that has now " two horses." Yet always we feel the unnatural calm and docility of the man, whom Carlyle saw as " a big fellow, soul and body, of many gifts (particularly in the Hogarth line with a dash of Sterne superadded), of enormous *appetite* withal and very uncertain and chaotic in all points except his *outer breeding*, which is fixed enough and *perfect* according to the modern English style. I rather dread explosions in his history. A big, fierce, weeping, hungry man."

The old Diogenes of letters needed no lantern when he saw a man. Big, fierce and hungry, Thackeray always was and always would be. And, at times, " weeping," but for what, not Carlyle nor any man, not even Thackeray himself, ever knew.

. . . . . .

The " spasms " grew worse, and *Lovel the Widower* appeared serially, in the *Cornhill*. Can it be that he was influenced by Dickens' example in using *Household Words* as the medium for telling his public all about his private differences with his wife, and the causes that led to their separation ?

For *Lovel the Widower* is no novel. Without a knowledge of Thackeray's life, it is practically meaningless. There are at least three " stories " in it, all overlapping and irrelevant, and characters so jumbled together and yet so unrelated that without the clue of his own life the book must seem some puzzling allegory.

At his worst, Thackeray could not have produced so bad a novel, even through illness, weariness, vanitarianism or love of money. But, as a last " broadside " at all those who had hurt his feelings or wounded his pride, it is a rather subtle sort of literary acrostic.

By constantly changing his own character with those of others and making them change theirs, he shows us people strangely akin to those of flesh and blood who had surrounded him during his life's journey – Fitzgerald; W. H. Brookfield and Mrs. Brookfield; the man who had swindled him into buying the *National Standard*; his own mother and his odious mother-in-law; and himself, as a widower, with children whose upbringing causes endless squabbling between their two grandmothers.

It is suggestive that Fitzgerald, the only man who had received Thackeray's confidences, could write of the book:

" . . . I don't think one can care much for Thackeray's novel. He is always talking so, of himself, too."

If any doubt remains, we need only read the bitter, rancorous " prologue " and the sly " epilogue " and the italics which add point to what is already sufficiently pointed.

" No, madam," he apostrophises Lady Baker; " it was your turn to bully me once – now it is mine, and I use it. No, you old catamaran, though you pretend you never read novels, some of your confounded good-natured friends will let you know of *this* one. Here you are, do you hear? Here you shall be shown up. And so I intend to show up *other* women and *other* men who have offended me."

And the dreary story drags on to its epilogue:

" *Valete et plaudite*, you good people who have witnessed the little comedy. . . . Good night, my little players. We have been merry together and we part with soft hearts and somewhat rueful countenances, don't we ? "

He said once to Mrs. Brookfield that no one could hit harder than he could, which was true. The pity of it was that he did not always scruple to look where he was hitting. As a result his methods of retaliation too often obscure the causes that prompted them. For, despite success and fame, he was really a lonely figure. Condemned to lifelong celibacy, he must never express any other reaction to it than grief for the loss of his wife. With a nature epicurean and kindly, he must always answer to the rigid test of temperance and devotion. Amused by the spectacle of human life, he must always sound a note of earnestness in depicting it. Sceptic in religious matters, he must always be thanking a genteel God for the pleasures of a circle he must always prefer to the society of his peers. A man of wit, he had been paid to " grin " ; of considerable honesty, he had been obliged to dissemble ; of some sensuality, he had been allowed only to admire. Born out of his century, he struggled to the height of a great figure in one that understood him but little, only to find in greatness a great loneliness.

The effect of such isolation and repression is to be found in his writing. More and more, as time went on, did his work become an outlet for the introspection produced by the thwarting of his instincts and inclinations, till in *Lovel the Widower* and *Philip* there is little else but himself.

Yet he had begun with *Barry Lyndon*, which is as objective a picture of a person and an age as can be read in any language. In *Vanity Fair*, the greatest picaresque novel in the English language, he is still a spectator of the world he limns. But with *Pendennis* he begins to look inwards, to revive for a while in *Esmond* and relapse again still more in *The Newcomes* and all his later work. More and more he becomes the hero of everything he writes, till with *Lovel the Widower* he finishes as the victim of everyone except himself.

And still, despite all blemishes, he could excel Scott at historical backgrounds, as easily as he could Dickens in characterisation ; and one suspects that, had he turned to history, he could have excelled Macaulay in vividness and surpassed him in liveliness, equalling him only in the bias of his outlook.

For Scott's history is archæology : every weapon, costume, castle and tourney has been authenticated before it is allowed to take its place on the orderly but over-precise stage upon which, at the given signal, enter the characters to act their parts.

With Thackeray, there is little direct description. He rings up no curtain upon a museum piece, but in some subtle way draws back the veil that hides the actual past, and we see it alive and bustling, not with heroes and heroines, but with real men and women, full of the contradiction of humanity, the absurdities, the mingled good and evil of live people whose final goal is the grave, not the wedding-bed.

Even his weakest characters, the Helens, Lauras and Amelias, he saves from the unreality of

Dickens, by spicing their virtues with a good deal of wholesome selfishness.

In the historical essay, though he is less informative than Macaulay, he is far more interpretative. He relies less on fact than on fancy, but it is an orderly fancy, a dramatisation of the figure he is describing, not merely an historical portrait.

For, indeed, his real powers lay in interpreting real people, not in creating imaginary ones. Truly he was neither novelist nor historian, but a subtle blend of both. Barry Lyndon was not a " creation " ; he was a dramatised interpretation of a real man, or of more than one, for he was in part founded upon Casanova, and in part upon a forgotten eighteenth-century blackguard whose history Thackeray had unearthed during the course of his wide but random researches into the past. Almost all the secondary characters of his novels, the lords and ladies, generals and statesmen, were real people whose history he had read and whom he brought to life through his extraordinary power of seeing dramatically the characters beneath the embalmed effigies of history.

He could do equally well the historical essay or the comedy of manners, and, at his best, could combine both. What he could not do was the conventional novel, of middle-class life, with a story and a moral. But this last was precisely what his generation asked him to do, and what, against his better judgment, he tried to do. He needed the discipline of established facts to keep his ebullient fancy within the bounds of artistry and taste. In biographical and historical studies he had such discipline, imposed by the facts and incidents of his subject. When laziness, illness, vanitarianism or dowries deflected him from his natural bent, he had no creative vein to fall back on. He turned to the nearest models he could find to draw from. Too often they were friends and relations and almost always he found himself among their number.

The *Widower* retired, to be followed by the limping *Philip*. But the editorial chair was cramping, private rancours nauseating, the " pavement sermons " intolerable. He resigned from the *Cornhill*. One more breath of the eighteenth century, or he would stifle ! One more gamble, not with the cards or dice of the Hon. Deuceace and Barry Lyndon, but with that genius that he threw so often and so recklessly, hoping for a " brace of mains."

He was commissioned to write a history of Queen Anne. It was a work after his own heart – work he should have given us if his literary integrity had equalled his great gifts. Queen Anne – not quite eighteenth century, but it contained the strip he wanted – Marlborough, the man who had always half fascinated and half repelled him ; Marlborough, the real rogue-hero of a picaresque novel – with half Europe for a " setting " ; for " plot " his fortunes, and as " price " any man living except himself. Here was a Barry Lyndon no one could quarrel with – a real historical rogue who would startle the virtue of middle-class England by showing them that if they would be virtuous they must expect virtue's own reward and leave " the glittering prizes " of the world to knaves – to the Marlboroughs, to Jack Churchill, the greatest general England ever had – a soldier who never ran from the enemy and never stood by a friend. It would not have been history, but it would have been Thackeray at his best, and Thackeray at his best is worth all the historians, saving only the inimitable Gibbon.

Something of his model's stature swelled his own. He would build a Queen Anne house in which to write his Queen Anne novel. The " pavement sermons " laid its foundations on Kensington Palace Green. It was to cost £6,000 and £100 ground rent. He would write his history of an age that knew its manners even if it had not published its morals, and write it in a gentleman's house – snob or no snob.

And then a Paris doctor told him that he had but a short while to live. True, a London doctor contradicted the first diagnosis, but between two such alternatives it is not always easy to believe the kinder. Thackeray seems to have accepted the first as the more probable, for to his publisher he said : " In which case good-bye Queen Anne, or rather, I shall see her sooner than I expected."

He was never afraid of death – and never hoped much from it. He knew life – found it a mixture, but on the whole goodish for a man of taste. He once wrote to his mother :

" I am well : Amen. I am ill : Amen. I die : Amen always. I can't say that having a tooth out is a blessing – is a punishment for my sins. I say it's having a tooth out."

A subversive philosophy for the age he lived in, but a comforting one for the time that was approaching. Now and again " the good pagan " shines through the veneer of an age that regarded religion as a social function in this world and an insurance policy for the next. To his old friend, Kate Perry, he had written, in 1856 :

" I don't think we deplore the old who have had enough of living and striving and have buried so many others and must be weary of living – it seems time for them to go – for where's the pleasure of staying when the feast is over, and the flowers withered and the guests gone ? Isn't it better to blow out the light than sit on among the broken meats and collapsed jellies and vapid heel-taps ? "

Lady Ritchie agrees, for she adds :
" Whenever my father wrote of death it was with peaceful encouragement and goodwill."

If ever he met Queen Anne hereafter – a consummation devoutly to be wished – he never wrote her history on this earth. It would take too long, and time was pressing, for of his daughters he wrote : " I have not made their fortunes yet, but I am getting towards it and have saved a little since I last wrote ; but I am free-handed, have to keep my wife, to help my parents, and to give to poor literary folk – in fine, my expenses are very large."

So he picked up his pen again, for *Denis Duval, Admiral of the White Squadron*. Back to the eighteenth century it must be, to old sea battles, oaths and grog – if need be, a cutlass or two – anything but an umbrella, and a prayer-book on a cushion. *Esmond* had been his card : *Duval* should be his epitaph. For the last time he tried to put to its full fastidious use the " beautiful vein of genius " that had lain " struggling about in him " while he struggled himself with indolence, ill health, vanities and dowries. From the fragment we have, we are teased with the feeling that we might have had another *Esmond*. But it is to be feared that, however long he had lived, we should never have had another *Vanity Fair*. The novel that made him famous made him cautious. Thereafter he thought less of fame than of success. In *Vanity Fair* he was thinking of neither. As a result it became his first success and remains his greatest claim to fame.

But *Denis Duval* was interrupted by the voice of a critic. Thackeray was not the victim this time. Too big, too famous, too hard a hitter, he was spared. His daughter, Anne, was the new quarry.

An anonymous critic in the *Athenæum* took her first novel, *The Story of Elizabeth*, read it, guffawed, tore it to shreds, and threw the pieces in her father's face.

Honour was satisfied, *Pendennis* avenged, and the shade of " bright, broken Maginn " looks back from beyond the Styx to see his most brilliant pupil struck across the face, as he had been taught to strike when young.

But the tired man made no answer. His name was wanted as a vice-president for the Shakespeare tercentenary. The invitation came from the man he had identified as the critic of his daughter's novel, and he declined to answer it. The silence produced a squabble, but still he made no answer.

A sacrifice was offered, and met with the cold reply that he had already driven one man out of a club and had no wish to do so with another. Despairingly, Shirley Brooks wrote to a friend :

" I wish that Thackeray would leave off caring about the snarls of these little Bohemian curs."

And, a while later, he did. On the morning of Christmas Eve, 1863, his valet found him in bed, body contracted, hands clasping the bed-rail. The most famous booth in Vanity Fair was empty.

BIBLIOGRAPHY

Pendennis, The Newcomes and *Lovel the Widower.*
Thackeray, by Anthony Trollope. English Men of Letters Series.
The Biographical Edition, 13 vols., published by Smith Elder. 1898–9. With a biographical introduction by Lady Ritchie.
Mrs. Brookfield and her Circle, by C. and F. Brookfield. London. 1905.
Bulwer : A Panorama – Edward and Rosina, by Michael Sadleir. London. 1931.
A Collection of Letters of W. M. Thackeray, 1847–1855. London. 1887.
Letters of Anne Thackeray Ritchie : with forty-two additional letters from her father, William Makepeace Thackeray. Selected and edited by her daughter, Hester Ritchie. 1924.
Thackeray : A Personality, by Malcolm Elwin. 1932.